THE BARBER OF SEVILLE

Gioacchino Rossini

1 7 9 2 - 1 8 6 8

Rosina . . . . Beverly Sills
Il Conte d'Almaviva . . . . Nicolai Gedda
Figaro . . . . Sherrill Milnes
Bartolo . . . . Renato Capecchi
Basilio . . . . Ruggero Raimondi
Berta . . . . Fedora Barbieri
Fiorello . . . . Joseph Galiano
Ambrogio/Uffizialer . . . . Michael Rippon

Conducted by James Levine
London Symphony Orchestra
John Alldis Choir
Chorus Master: John Alldis

THE BARBER OF SEVILLE

THE BARBER
OF SEVILLE

Gioacchino Rossini

TEXT BY DAVID FOIL

Additional commentary by William Berger

BLACK **D**OG
& **L**EVENTHAL
PUBLISHERS
NEW YORK

Published by
Black Dog & Leventhal Publishers, Inc.
151 West 19th Street
New York, NY 10011

Distributed by
Workman Publishing Company
708 Broadway
New York, NY 10003

Manufactured in China

Cover and interior design by Liz Driesbach.

Cover image: Thenard playing Figaro by Henri-Pierre Danloux (1753-1809)
Comedie Francaise/Bridgeman Art Library

ISBN 10: 1-57912-618-9
ISBN 13: 978-157912-618-6

h g f e d c b a

Library of Congress Cataloging-in-Publication Data available on file.

The Barber of Seville is perhaps the most important and influential comedic opera in the modern repertoire. It is truly a masterpiece—for its composer and its genre in terms of structure, form and content. But, at the same time, it can only be so because it is so full of exciting, fun, beautiful music. An *opera buffa* in the classic sense, *The Barber of Seville* is dynamic without being confusing, funny without being preposterous, touching without being melodramatic and full of some of the most fantastic music in nineteenth-century opera.

Enjoy this book and enjoy the music.

ABOUT THE AUTHOR

David Foil is the author of the six-volume Black Dog Music Library and the first four volumes of the Black Dog Opera Library. A native of Lousiana, he has written extensively about music, theater and film both as a critic for newspapers in the South and as an annotator for a wide range of classical recordings for the Angel/EMI classics, Columbia and Sony Classical labels. He lives in New York City.

THE BARBER
OF SEVILLE

*W*hen he was an old man, the Jupiter of Italian opera, Giuseppe Verdi, was moved to write to a friend, "I confess that I cannot help believing *Il Barbiere di Siviglia,* for abundance of ideas, for comic verve, and for truth of declamation, the most beautiful *opera buffa* in existence." Since Verdi was not given to hyperbole, his words spin and dazzle like the greatest compliment in the history of music. Verdi knew what he was talking about: when he wrote these words in 1898, he had already composed his miraculous, quicksilver *Falstaff,* as perfect and elegant a comic opera as one can imagine. But *Falstaff* was a different kind of comedy, like Mozart's *The Marriage of Figaro*

Gioacchino Rossini (1792-1868)

and Wagner's *Die Meistersinger von Nürnberg*—a human comedy, just a heartbeat away from tragedy, its radiant humor and high spirits streaked with shadow and melancholy. *Opera buffa* is another matter, silly, giddy and uproarious by comparison. And, as Verdi suggested, there is no argument that Giaocchino Rossini's *Il Barbiere di Siviglia* is its ideal.

The Italian word *buffa* means "puff" or "gust." When it is used to describe an opera, it suggests the kind of breathless comedy we might call madcap, screwball, or slapstick—maybe all three, at once. Think of a Marx Brothers movie, one of the *Pink Panther* series with Peter Sellers, or a memorable episode of *I Love Lucy*; that is buffa comedy. Rossini wrote in this style better and more consistently than any other composer. He wrote other inspired buffa comedies, such as *La Cenerentola, L'Italiana in Algeri, Il Turco in Italia, Il Viaggio a Reims and Le Comte Ory*. But none of them sparkles and delights quite like *Il Barbiere di Siviglia* (which we'll now refer to as *The Barber of Seville*).

Part of the charm is the story itself. It is drawn from the hugely popular stage comedy of the

Pierre Auguste Caron
De Beaumarchais (1732-1799)

same name by the French playwright Beaumarchais (1732- 99), a man whose fortunes rose and fell repeatedly as a financial speculator, secret agent, gun-runner and man of letters who even had a significant hand in French involvement in the American Revolution. At least as fascinating as his own characters, Beaumarchais (whose real name was Pierre Augustin Caron) wrote a trilogy of deftly satirical comedies that followed the relationships of a group of characters from both the servant class and the nobility—*Le Barbier de Seville, Le Mariage de Figaro* and *La Mère Coupable.* In pre-Revolutionary Paris, the political impact of the first two plays was considerable. The character of Figaro, the barber of Seville who gets married in its sequel, is a gifted and wily man (not unlike Beaumarchais) who is passionate about the idea of personal freedom and individual dignity. But he is trapped in a society where a man like his master, Count Almaviva, always has the upper hand. The buoyant *Barbier de Seville* was a stage triumph in Paris in 1775. Six years later, though, Louis XVI was so offended by the impertinence of the more critical *Mariage de Figaro* that he banned it outright, and it was not performed for several years.

Beaumarchais' first play tells how the resourceful Figaro helps Count Almaviva win the hand of the beautiful Rosina, who becomes the Countess in the second play. The playwright planned *Le Barbier de Seville* as a comic opera, possibly using songs he had collected during a visit to Spain. His libretto was rejected by the Opéra Comique in Paris. An operatic version did emerge, though, in St. Petersburg in 1782, written by the Italian composer Giovanni Paisiello, who was then Catherine the Great's music master. Paisiello's *Barbiere di Siviglia* was a great success and became a staple of the European repertoire of comic operas. (Mozart's opera of *Le Mariage de Figaro,* in Italian, followed in 1786.) When Rossini approached the idea of writing his own opera of *Le Barbier de Seville* in 1816, the popularity of Paisiello's version concerned him, and some accounts suggest that he sought Paisiello's blessing.

But there was no copyright law at the time, and the popular play was fair game. In addition to the Paisiello, there were no less than five other operatic versions of Beaumarchais' play written between its premiere and the first performance of Rossini's opera. The libretto for Rossini's *Barber of Seville,* by Cesare Sterbini, is a shrewd adaptation of the play (with a fair amount of borrowing from Paisiello's libretto) that emphasizes the story's screwball elements, but not its political satire. It is a fine framework for a comic opera. But the genius in *The Barber of Seville* is Rossini's. Inspired by his libretto, the composer provided music that never fails to disarm and delight, almost two centuries later. The score is inexhaustibly tuneful, deft and magical in its expressive skill, and as sensuous and effervescent as a fine champagne. Most of all, it sparkles with Rossini's inimitable musical wit. He was a fine composer of dramatic operas, but his sense of comedy was incomparable. No other composer could make music laugh and smile so winningly, not even Mozart.

And here is the most amazing fact: Rossini did it all in less than a month.

The Barber of Seville had its premiere in Rome on February 20, 1816, at the Teatro Argentina during the Carnival season.

By all accounts, the 22-year-old Rossini did not even receive the libretto to begin work until the last week of January. He had started the 1815-16 season in Naples, where he was under contract to direct the theaters and compose a number of new operas for the season. The first of them was the serious opera *Elisabetta, Regina d'Inghilterra* (Elizabeth, Queen of England), which had its premiere on October 4 at the city's Teatro San Carlo. Rossini's Neopolitan contract allowed him some freedom, though. He took advantage of it to accept an invitation to spend the late fall and early winter in Rome. In addition to writing another serious opera, *Torvaldo e Dorliska*, and supervising a new production of his *Il Turco in Italia* at the Teatro Valle in November and December, he agreed to write a pair of lighter works for the pre-Lenten Carnival season that followed, under the patronage of the Duke of Sforza-Cesarini, who owned and operated the Teatro Argentina.

All of this sounds grand and a bit glamorous in retrospect; in reality, it proved to be an ordeal verging on catastrophe.

A 1982 production of *Barber* at the Metropolitan Opera in New York.

Control of Rome had just been returned to the Vatican, with the collapse of the Napoleonic Empire. Papal authorities chose to administer the city's theaters with an iron and censorious hand, slashing the subsidy granted them by the Napoleonic government. While audiences loved *Il Turco in Italia, Torvaldo e Dorliska* was a fiasco in its premiere on December 26, 1815. Rossini was probably glad to have the Teatro Argentina commission to follow it. But the situation that greeted him was dire. To make ends meet there, the Duke was forced to plan a crowd-pleasing season of comic opera. He had such a difficult time gathering his ensemble that he was forced to stage Rossini's *L'Italiana in Algeri*—already old hat, having been written two-and-a-half years earlier—in order to open by mid-January. The conditions were gruelling. Contemporary accounts reveal that the Teatro Argentina was a dingy, filthy and uncomfortable place, typical of Roman theaters of the day. To get *L'Italiana in Algeri* on its feet, Rossini and his singers endured agonizing rehearsals in unheated rooms in the damp chill of the Roman winter. As if the situation were not grim enough already, the utterly exhausted 44-year-old Duke of Sforza-Cesarini died suddenly of a stroke in the early morning hours of February 7, 1816, the day after Rossini delivered the completed score for Act I of his new comic opera. It was in this atmosphere of seething tension, personal discomfort, budgetary nightmares and sudden death that he wrote *The Barber of Seville*—or what later became *The Barber of Seville*. When the opera had its premiere, it was entitled *Almaviva o sia L'Inutile Precauzione* (Almaviva, or The Futile Precaution), perhaps because of Rossini's fear of offending Paisiello and the fans of his opera. (Almost 60 years later, Verdi would similarly wonder whether he should retitle his *Otello as Iago*, because of the high regard he and others had for Rossini's version of *Otello*.) Compromises such as this were common for composers then. Rossini spun out his operas in much the same way a writer today whips out a script for a TV series—fast, furiously and with whatever he could put to good use. He cheerfully borrowed from himself to fill in here and there, and he left the writing of the recitatives to someone else. Despite all the privation that surrounded him, Rossini seems to have been in good spirits when he composed the opera. He was surrounded by a fine cast that pulled together in a desperate situation, and it is difficult to listen to the music and not imagine Rossini laughing as he wrote. The most convincing accounts suggest that a total of 24 days elapsed between the conception of *The Barber of Seville* and its premiere. At best, Rossini had a little more than two weeks to actually compose the music, which amounted to 600 pages of manuscript. Scholars have tracked down the many places in the score for *The Barber of Seville* where he stole from his own earlier works, usually just a melody or a phrase. Some have found echoes of Haydn and Spontini in the score, and even a Russian folk song.

The most famous contingency in the score for *The Barber of Seville,* though, is its most famous feature—the overture. Rossini apparently wrote an original overture for the opera but it was lost. In its place, he used an overture that had already served him not once but twice in earlier operas, both of them dramas—*Aureliano in Pamira* and *Elisabetta, Regina d'Inghilterra,* for which he added some military-sounding embellishments.

He removed those for *The Barber of Seville,* where the overture came to rest finally and fortuitously. It is an ironic twist, for the bustling overture seems the perfect embodiment of the intrigue, slapstick and buoyant good will of *The Barber of Seville,* crowned by one of Rossini's thrilling, trademark crescendos. After all this frantic preparation, the opening

Dame Nellie Melba (1861-1931) as Rosina

night was a disaster. Murphy's Law hit overdrive. Topping off a performance filled with more than its share of gaffes and miscues, an itinerant cat padded onto the stage during the finale, mingling with the frazzled cast and leaving the indifferent audience hysterical with laughter and meowing at the cat as the singers bravely tried to do their job. Geltrude Righetti-Georgi, a childhood friend of Rossini's who came out of retirement to create the role of Rosina, reported that the composer was devastated, and who could blame him? Curiously, as was the case with the Beaumarchais play (which also opened to derision), the public response completely reversed itself in a matter of days. *The Barber of Seville* delighted its second audience, and its appeal has grown ever since.

Such a story tells us a lot about the composer and the musical world he inhabited. In our time, Rossini is a much misunderstood composer because he does not conform to our idea of an artist. Though he lived to the age of 75, he essentially retired when he was 37, after composing nearly 40 operas. He was rich, happy and universally beloved, and he simply decided to enjoy the rest of his life in luxurious comfort, first in Bologna, then in Paris where he became the merry *eminence grise* of musical life. The photos we have of Rossini come from this period, and you can see in his face just how content he was—a slight smile, a light in his eyes, an air of well-being, crowning a stout figure that bespeaks the good life. (There is an obvious reason why the gourmet dish known as tournedos Rossini came into being.) He was, first and foremost, a man of the theater, with a shrewd sense of how to please an audience. Perhaps, in 1829, Rossini sensed the coming revolution in opera, signaled by the innovations of Weber and Meyerbeer, later fully realized by the genius of Verdi and Wagner. His last opera, *William Tell*, is one of his masterpieces, a noble and stupendous work that definitely points to the future—Wagnerian in its scope and dimensions, Verdian in its incisive characterization and narrative.

But Rossini was an entertainer, not a philosopher, and he was just the kind of figure the emerging Romantic era would find a bit foolish and passé. He wrote operas to make money, as much money as he could possibly negotiate, and he needed money to support himself in the style he desired. His operas have a patented sound; as we have seen, they frequently even share bits of the same music. There are French and Italian versions of several of his operas, because he was happy to adapt them variously to meet the demands of the moment. (Verdi would have to do the same thing, though a good deal less cheerfully.) Rossini believed himself to be an artist but also a showman, and he barely dreamed of the kind of artistic autonomy Verdi and Wagner would one day expect as their due. It simply did not exist in his world, as it did not exist in Mozart's. Would he have liked it? Certainly. But he seemed to know that his time had passed, and he graciously passed into legend, a status he enjoyed immensely.

Aside from the brilliance of the work itself, the reason for the consistent popularity of *The Barber of Seville* has been its popularity with singers. The original cast boasted a bona fide legend—the Spanish tenor Manuel Garcia, who created the role of Count Almaviva and made a specialty of it. Garcia later became the most famous voice teacher of his day and was the first to develop and teach a technique for vocal development. He was also the father of two legendary singers, Maria Malibran and Pauline Viardot-Garcia. One of the most beautiful and entrancing divas of what we now call the bel canto era, Malibran once sang Rosina to her father's Almaviva, but she died tragically young. Viardot-Garcia was a comparatively homely woman, but she became an equally famous singer in Paris in the mid-19th century. She was also brilliant, with a compelling personality, and she was almost as potent a figure in Parisian musical society as Rossini himself. He invited her to sing the mezzo-soprano solos in the first, private performance of portions of his setting of the *Stabat Mater*.

Pauline Viardot-Garcia, 1893

Vocal styles changed a great deal after Rossini's retirement. He understood the voice very well, even if his writing tested the limits of what singers could do. But the elegant, graceful style of singing he and his contemporaries Bellini and Donizetti knew and catered to—*bel canto*, it was later dubbed—was undergoing a transformation. Singing had to become more forceful, more pungent and simply louder, to accommodate the demands of Romantic opera. As a composer, Rossini had an unpleasant taste of this after the premiere of *William Tell*. Tenors had just begun then to develop the technique of singing their high notes with chest resonance, instead of projecting them in a lighter "head" voice that almost sounds like a falsetto. Rossini was skeptical. When he heard the tenor Gilbert Duprez sing the tenor aria from *William Tell* with trumpeted high C's sung from the chest, he was aghast, reportedly describing the sound as that of "a capon having its head cut off." Years later, the young soprano Adelina Patti—the greatest diva of the latter half of the 19th century—came to one of Rossini's famous *musicales* in Paris and sang Rosina's "Una voce poco fa" from *The Barber of Seville*, with her own elaborate embellishments. Rossini was appalled, and he devastated Patti by sarcastically wondering aloud who had written the piece she had just sung. The composer Camille Saint-Saëns wrote that, days later, Rossini was still fuming about the incident. He told Saint-Saëns that, while some decoration of the vocal line was to be expected, Patti had made the aria unrecognizable. In the same conversation, he complained about the growing attraction sopranos had for the role of Rosina, which he had intended for a mezzo-soprano—an attraction that persists to this day.

The legacy of all this makes *The Barber of Seville* an irresistible but in some ways elusive opera in the modern world, despite the attraction of the music. The recording included with this book was the first truly complete recording of the score. The singing is definitely on the modern scale: Rossini might have been non-plussed by the booming splendor of Sherrill Milnes' Figaro and the crisp, ringing sound of tenor Nicolai Gedda's Almaviva. The recording also departs from strict historical accuracy, as the composer might have complained, by featuring a lyric soprano as Rosina. But Beverly Sills (who was the primary reason for this recording) was following a long tradition of sopranos singing the role. From Patti forward, it has been as much a staple for such sopranos as Luisa Tetrazzini, Amelita Galli-Curci, Toti dal Monte, Lina Pagliughi, Lily Pons, Roberta Peters, Kathleen Battle and Ruth Ann Swenson. At the same time, mezzo-sopranos such as Conchita Supervia, Giulietta Simionato, Teresa Berganza, Marilyn Horne, Frederica von Stade, Suzanne Mentzer, Cecilia Bartoli, Jennifer Larmore and Vesselina Kasarova have had brilliant successes in the role, as well.

In the end, these are just details in the service of genius. Rossini's fame and popularity might have been eclipsed by Verdi, Wagner, Puccini and others. We might view his operas with polite fascination, as splendid objects from another time and place, fabulous and transcendently beautiful antiques. But *The Barber of Seville* endures, evergreen and perfect, a comedy that merrily defies the passage of time. After almost 200 years of relentless performances, if you listen carefully through the music, you might still hear Rossini laughing.

THE STORY OF THE OPERA

Act 1

SCENE ONE

It is early morning in the Spanish city of Seville, and the first rays of sunlight spread across a sleepy square to the outside walls of the home of Don Bartolo. The servant Fiorello beckons a group of musicians-for-hire into the square, where they quietly prepare to play. With them is Count Almaviva, and they accompany him in a morning serenade beneath the window of Rosina, the lovely young ward of Don Bartolo. In his song, the Count beckons Rosina to end his torment and surrender to his love. But Rosina does not seem to have heard the him. He abandons his serenade, telling Fiorello to pay the musicians and send them away. The musicians are a little too noisy in expressing their gratitude, and it takes both the Count and Fiorello to get rid of them without disturbing the neighbors. The Count has not given up hope that Rosina will appear. He lingers in the square until he hears a raucous voice in the distance, which causes him to run for cover. The singer is Figaro, the indefatigable barber (and factotum, or know-it-all) of Seville going about his business. Figaro savors his amazing ability to be all things to all people, all of the time. The Count emerges from his hiding place when he realizes it is his subject Figaro, who is astonished to see his master under such circumstances. The nobleman swears Figaro to secrecy and tells the servant he is infatuated with the beautiful Rosina, whom he has been following since he first saw her in Madrid. Always in the know, Figaro is able to fill in the details for the Count...after all, Figaro is a frequent visitor to Don Bartolo's home. Their chat is interrupted when Rosina emerges on the balcony. She carries with her a letter. Before she and the Count can find each other, Bartolo joins her to greet the morning; seeing the letter, he demands to know what it says. Just the words of an aria from a romantic opera called *The Futile Precaution,* she slyly tells Bartolo, as she lets the letter slip from her fingers to the street below. Bartolo is appalled by her indiscreet taste in opera and heads for the street to find the page, though the Count beats him to it. Suspecting a ruse, Bartolo hustles Rosina back into the house. When Figaro reads the letter to the Count, it reveals Rosina's interest. But, it asks, could she know who he is and what he intends? The Count's joy is short-lived, for Bartolo emerges from his home, bursting with the news that he is to marry Rosina later that day. As he leaves to finalize the plans, Figaro and the Count decide another serenade is in order. He informs her in his song that he is the poor but ardent Lindoro. She is charmed and responds to him, singing from behind the shutters of her rooms, though she suddenly breaks off. The Count is elated. Can Figaro help him get into the house? The servant's ears

immediately perk up when he learns there will be a handsome reward for him. Figaro tells the Count that a regiment is expected in town, led by a colonel he knows, and that he can arrange for Bartolo to be required to billet the troops, which could include the disguised Count. Figaro suggests his lord act like a drunkard, for good measure, since Bartolo is less inclined to suspect a man in such a condition. They agree to meet at Figaro's shop to seal the deal—the Count a lover fulfilled, Figaro a little richer in the bargain.

SCENE TWO

In the courtyard of Bartolo's house, Rosina is holding yet another response to Lindoro. She is determined to be with him, in spite of Bartolo's ridiculous expectations, and she begins plotting how to make it happen. With the exquisite timing that is his alone, Figaro turns up just as she is pondering her problem. But before they can discuss a solution, Bartolo enters, fuming at Figaro that the barber/surgeon's cures and remedies have only succeeded in making the entire household sick: the servants Berta and Ambrogio can't stop yawning and sneezing. Rosina has slipped away in the midst of this encounter, but her music teacher Don Basilio suddenly arrives. He can't wait to tell Bartolo that his rival for Rosina's hand—Count Almaviva—has been spotted in Seville. Basilio calms Bartolo with the assurance that he can handle the situation, through the devilish workings of calumny. Bartolo decides to rush the marriage contract; Basilio is happy to oblige, if the price is right. Figaro has overheard all of this and tells Rosina. She wants to know who it was she saw Figaro with earlier. His poor cousin, he tells her, who is dying of love for none other than her. He tells her that Lindoro only needs a line or two from her to convince him of her love. She sends Figaro off with the letter written earlier. Bartolo enters, full of suspicions about Figaro, the ink stains of Rosina's fingers, a missing sheet of paper...Rosina tries to explain, but Bartolo is not fooled. He doubles the guard on her door and both leave in a fury. Berta answers a knock at the door. The Count enters, in disguise and playing the drunkard. He presents Bartolo with his billet, scanning the room for a sign of Rosina. An angry Bartolo looks for the papers that exempt him from billeting troops, while Rosina appears and the drunken soldier reveals himself to her as Lindoro. A comedy of errors ensues: Bartolo finds the exemption, the Count knocks it out of his hand while he passes a note to Rosina, which she exchanges for a laundry list before Bartolo can demand to see it. She begins to cry at Bartolo's anger, the Count berates Bartolo, and Berta enters with Basilio to add to the confusion. The sudden but timely arrival of Figaro calms the scene momentarily, until the real billeted soldiers arrive, joined by curious neighbors drawn by the disturbance. The officer leading the regiment is about to arrest the Count as an imposter, until the Count shows him a document that draws from the officer a salute. Everyone begins to wonder aloud about the insane turn of events, which is so bizarre that it has them all spellbound and completely frazzled.

Act 2

That masquerading "soldier" has vanished, of course, but Bartolo is sure he was an agent of Count Almaviva. Bartolo's inquiries have yielded nothing. He is in the music room of his house, planning his next step, when a knock at the door announces one Don Alonso, an unexpected guest who is, in fact, the Count in yet another disguise. Bartolo does not recognize him but is still suspicious. Alonso tells Bartolo that he is a student of Basilio's, whom he says is ill; Alonso has come to give Rosina her voice lesson. What's more, he presents to Bartolo Rosina's letter to the Count, which he says he can use to make Rosina think the Count is faithless. Such a scheme proves to Bartolo that Alonso is indeed Basilio's student, and he brings Rosina in for her lesson. She recognizes her Lindoro immediately, though she reveals this to him secretly, by choosing the aria from *The Futile Precaution* for her voice lesson. Alonso praises Rosina's voice, but Bartolo is appalled by the brazenness of the aria. He suggests something more discreet, which he demonstrates, as Figaro enters and mimics him behind his back. Bartolo wheels on Figaro, wanting to know why he has arrived. To give Bartolo a shave, of course,

Figaro tells him. Bartolo reluctantly goes to find towels, when Figaro asks Rosina for the key to the outside window. Suspicious of Figaro, Bartolo returns and sends the barber himself to get the towels. Figaro stages a diversion, sending Bartolo running out of the room, and that allows him to return with the correct key for the Count. Then Basilio turns up, and the whole ruse threatens to collapse until the Count bribes the music teacher, who leaves happy with his bag of gold coins. Figaro resumes shaving Bartolo, and the Count tells Rosina he will meet her that night. But Bartolo overhears the plan and chases them all away in a rage. The tired old servant Berta complains about the noise but realizes that love is behind it all and that even she is susceptible to its allure. Bartolo re-enters with Basilio, who is convinced Alonso was actually the Count. When he learns Figaro is searching for a notary for the marriage of his "niece," Bartolo tries to head him off by sending Basilio to obtain the notary instead. But he is not finished: Bartolo still has Rosina's letter, which Alonso gave him, and he uses it to convince Rosina that the Count/Lindoro is faithless. She is devastated, and she explains the whole plot to the grimly satisfied Bartolo. A storm shatters the evening calm but it fades in time for Figaro and the Count to slip over the wall for their rescue of Rosina. She is furious with her beloved, whom she now believes has deceived her. Lindoro calms her by explaining that he is Count Almaviva. Figaro tries to speed the reconciled lovers over the wall, only to discover their ladder has been removed. They hide. Basilio arrives with the notary, but the Count intervenes. He makes Basilio an offer he cannot refuse: to witness the signing of the contract, only by Rosina and the Count. Bartolo has soldiers with him when he bursts in to stop the marriage, but he is outclassed, outstripped and outranked by the Count. The old man finally gives up but feels a bit better when the Count offers him a handsome dowry for Rosina's hand. The Count, Rosina and the newly enriched Figaro exult in their triumph, and everyone joins them in best wishes for the happily-ever-after future of the Count and his new Countess.

THE BARBER OF SEVILLE

Gioacchino Rossini
1792 - 1868

Rosina . . . . Beverly Sills
Il Conte d'Almaviva . . . . Nicolai Gedda
Figaro . . . . Sherrill Milnes
Bartolo . . . . Renato Capecchi
Basilio . . . . Ruggero Raimondi
Berta . . . . Fedora Barbieri
Fiorello . . . . Joseph Galiano
Ambrogio/Uffizialer . . . . Michael Rippon

Conducted by James Levine
London Symphony Orchestra
John Alldis Choir
Chorus Master: John Alldis

THE PERFORMERS

BEVERLY SILLS (Rosina) has been perhaps one of the most popular and influential American musicians of the 20th century. Born in Brooklyn as Belle Miriam Silverman, she was the daughter of immigrants, an insurance salesman and a woman with musical interests who put her in show business as a baby. At the age of 3, she won a radio contest in Brooklyn as "the most beautiful baby of 1932." Nicknamed "Bubbles," she grew up singing in commercials and performing on the radio. Her vocal studies began when she was 7, as a student of Estelle Liebling, and she made her operatic debut at the Philadelphia Civic Opera in 1947 as Frasquita in a production of *Carmen*. Sills built her career without going to Europe—almost unheard of for a serious American singer in the 1950s—singing with a number of important American opera companies, including the San Francisco Opera in 1953 and, two years later, the New York City Opera. She would remain on the New York City Opera roster for the next 25 years, during which the company emerged from the shadow of the more glamorous Metropolitan

Beverly Sills and her daughter, who is deaf.

Opera and established its own artistic identity. With conductor Julius Rudel, Sills was a key element in that transformation, a singing actress of formidable skill and wide-ranging virtuosity who led the company's superb and loyal ensemble of American singers. Her repertoire was all-embracing, a testament to her intelligence, musicianship and passion. She memorably created the title role in Douglas Moore's *The Ballad of Baby Doe* and even sang in American performances of Luigi Nono's post-serialist opera *Intolleranza*. But her true metier was in 19th-century opera, primarily Italian *bel canto* and French roles. Her voice was essentially a lyric soprano, with great flexibility and range, though she enjoyed some of her great successes in more dramatic roles. In 1966 at City Opera, she had a career breakthrough as Cleopatra in Handel's *Julius Caesar*, and she became increasingly more identified with the revival of interest in *bel canto* opera. Along with Dame Joan

Sutherland and Montserrat Caballé, she championed the operas of Bellini, Donizetti and Rossini, putting her own personal stamp on the leading roles in *Lucia di Lammermoor, Norma, Don Pasquale, La Fille du Regiment, L'Assedio di Corinto* and Donizetti's "Tudor queen trilogy"—*Anna Bolena, Maria Stuarda* and *Roberto Devereux*. She also triumphed in the title role of Massenet's *Manon,* as the three heroines of Offenbach's *Les contes d'Hoffmann* and as Violetta in *La Traviata*. Sills' career went international in the late 1960s with successful debuts at Teatro Colón in Buenos Aires, Deutsche Oper in Berlin and La Scala in Milan. Her Metropolitan Opera debut came, at the height of her fame, in 1975 as Pamira in *L'Assedio di Corinto*. Throughout the 1970s, she was known as America's "queen of opera," appearing frequently on TV and enjoying a belated international recording career. Following her retirement, Sills served with distinction as general director of New York City Opera, from which she retired in 1988, and she later served as chair of Lincoln Center for the Performing Arts.

NICOLAI GEDDA (Almaviva/Lindoro) has become the model of the modern tenor, equally at home on opera, recital and concert stages, a sophisticated singer equipped with a firm but flexible technique that has allowed him to encompass a repertoire almost unprecedented in its breadth. He was born in Stockholm in 1925 to a Swedish mother and a Russian father (who was a bass in the Don Cossack Choir) and spent part of his childhood in Leipzig. His gift for languages was a key factor in his early success, making his professional debut in

Stockholm in 1952 in the title role of Adam's *Le Postillon de Longjumeau*. Walter Legge of EMI Records happened to hear Gedda during a Stockholm visit that year and, noting his linguistic skill as well as his brilliant lyric tenor voice, immediately signed him for an upcoming recording of *Boris Godunov*. Major European debuts followed quickly, as Gedda established himself with a succession of important recordings for EMI. In addition to opera, he was recognized as a distinguished lieder singer and oratorio soloist. After his Metropolitan Opera debut in 1957, he created the title role in the company's world premiere of Samuel Barber's *Vanessa* the following year. For the next 30 years, Gedda sang operatic roles as diverse as the boyish Nemorino in *L'Elisir d'amore* and the heroic title part in Wagner's *Lohengrin*. Later in his career, he took on Russian roles and explored unusual areas of the song repertoire, with occasional forays into novelty like composer-conductor Leonard Bernstein's definitive recording of his musical *Candide*.

SHERRILL MILNES (Figaro) has been an important link in the 20th-century tradition that one pundit has called "the prairie baritone"—an American baritone with a big, powerful, richly dark sound, with ringing high notes and a self-confidence that almost has a cowboy's swagger. When he came on the scene in mid-1960s, Milnes joined a line of baritones that included Lawrence Tibbett, John Charles Thomas, Leonard Warren and Robert Merrill, and also inspired such pop singers as John Raitt, Howard Keel and Gordon MacRae. Milnes was born in Downers Grove, Illinois, and decided to become a singer after beginning a medical degree. He studied at Drake University and Northwestern University, and sang in choral performances in the Chicago area. After apprenticing at the Santa Fe Opera, Milnes joined teacher/director Boris Goldovsky's opera ensemble in 1960 and, the following year, met the retired diva Rosa Ponselle. Ponselle coached him in several roles and, at Baltimore Civic Opera, sponsored his debut as Carlo Gérald in *Andrea Chénier*. He made his European debut in 1964 as Figaro in *The Barber of Seville* at Milan's Teatro Nuovo, but returned to the U.S. almost immediately to make his New York City Opera debut as Valentin in *Faust*. His Metropolitan Opera debut, again as Valentin, came on December 22, 1965, beginning a relationship that would stretch over three decades. As Robert Merrill's stage career at the Met came to an end, Milnes assumed many of his signature roles, with particular acclaim in such Verdi operas as *Rigoletto, La Traviata, Un Ballo in Maschera, Aida, Don Carlo, Il Trovatore, I Vespri Siciliani, Simon Boccanegra* and *Otello* as well as Valentin, Rossini's Figaro, as Carlo Gérard and in baritone roles in *La Gioconda, Pagliacci, La Fanciulla del West* and *Thaïs*. During the 1970s, Milnes was a mainstay at the Met, as well as the most celebrated American and international companies, and he recorded extensively, often with tenor Plácido Domingo. In the 1990s, Milnes began concentrating on leading character roles such as Amonasro in *Aida* and Scarpia in *Tosca,* and even the title role in Verdi's *Falstaff.*

RENATO CAPECCHI (Don Bartolo) enjoyed an uncommonly long career as baritone, first in leading lyric and Verdi roles, then as a character singer. Born in Cairo to Italian parents, he studied voice in Milan and made his stage debut in 1948 at Reggio Emilia, as Amonasro in *Aida.* Capecchi joined the La Scala company in 1950 and bowed the following year at the Metropolitan Opera as Giorgio Germont in *La Traviata.* He later made a notable appearance in the title role of *Don Giovanni* at the Aix-en-Provence festival, but enjoyed an even more telling success in 1955 as Don Bartolo in *The Barber of Seville* at the Arena di Verona. This signaled the beginning of his career as an impeccable buffa singer, his fine voice allied with a wonderful comic sense and solid stage skills. Capecchi was also memorable as Fra Melitone in *La Forza del Destino,* the title roles in *Falstaff* (in which he also sang the role of Ford) and *Gianni Schicchi, Don Pasquale* and even *The Barber of Seville,* in which he was a celebrated Figaro. He also sang the role of Figaro in Mozart's *The Marriage of Figaro,* as well as both Sgt. Belcore and Dr. Dulcamara in *L'Elisir d'amore.*

RUGGERO RAIMONDI (Don Basilio) has been one of the finest singing actors of his generation, enjoying a career of distinction, particularly in Mozart and Verdi, virtually since he began

singing professionally. Born in Bologna in 1941 and educated at Rome's Accademia di Santa Cecilia, the Italian bass made his debut in 1964 at the Spoleto Festival as Colline in Puccini's *La Bohème*. He joined the roster at Milan's La Scala three years later, with his Metropolitan Opera debut following in the fall of 1970, as Silva in *Ernani*. Raimondi has won particular acclaim for his portrayals of King Philip II in *Don Carlo*, Figaro in *The Marriage of Figaro* and the title roles in *Don Giovanni* and *Boris Godunov*. The suave, theatrical intensity of his performances has been a career trademark, to such a degree that conductor Herbert von Karajan convinced him to undertake the nominally baritone role of Scarpia—in a tour de force portrayal of uncommonly sinister elegance—for the maestro's final recording of *Tosca*. Raimondi has also triumphed in two internationally acclaimed film versions of operas, as Escamillo in Francesco Rosi's *Carmen* (1984) and in the title role of

Joseph Losey's *Don Giovanni* (1979). His film performances were so successful that he went on to act in non-musical Italian films. But opera, both on the stage and in recordings, has been his true metier, in a career remarkable for its breadth and consistency, paralleling that of his frequent colleague, tenor Plácido Domingo.

FEDORA BARBIERI (Berta) was in the twilight of her career when she made this recording, taking a role usually sung by a comprimario because of the inclusion of the maid's rarely performed aria. Barbieri was one of the leading Italian mezzo-sopranos of the 1940s and 1950s—following in the distinctive tradition of such great mezzo divas as Lina Bruna Rasa and Ebe Stignani—best known to most listeners for memorably partnering Maria Callas in classic recordings of *Aida* (as Amneris) and *Il Trovatore* (as Azucena). A native of Trieste, she made her professional debut in Florence in 1940, at the age of 20, singing throughout Europe during the early years of World War II. She briefly retired after marrying in 1943, but returned to the stage in Florence in 1945 with a portrayal of Azucena that signaled the emergence of a major talent. Barbieri's international career blossomed in the late 1940s to include regular visits to the major companies in Paris, Vienna, London, Buenos Aires, New York, San Francisco and Chicago, and she enjoyed a long, distinguished affiliation with La Scala in Milan. She sang most of the leading mezzo-soprano and contralto roles in Italian opera and was also acclaimed for her performance in the title role of *Carmen*.

James Levine has been a dominant figure in the world of opera in the last quarter of the 20th century, both as a versatile conductor and as the vigorous artistic leader of the Metropolitan Opera at a decisive stage in its history. He has become the model of the modern maestro, formidably and prodigiously talented, indefatigable, ambitious and at home at the helm of any of the world's best orchestras and opera companies. Born in Cincinnati in 1943 to a pop musician and an actress, Levine was a child prodigy who studied piano with Rudolf Serkin and Rosina Lhevinne before entering the Julliard School of Music in 1961. His first coaching as a conductor came at Julliard from Jean Morel, and he also studied with Wolfgang Vacano at the Aspen Festival. After an early apprenticeship in Baltimore, Levine spent five years as an assistant conductor to George Szell at the Cleveland Orchestra. In 1970, his career expanded through conducting debuts with the Philadelphia Orchestra, Welsh National Opera and San Fransisco Opera. In June of 1971, at the age of 27, he conducted a Metropolitan Opera performance for the first time—an outdoor post-season *Tosca*. Further appearances during the following subscription season led to his appointment as the company's first principal conductor. As the management structure of the Met began to change, Levine began to assume more responsibility, taking over as music director in 1975, after Rafael Kubelik's resignation. His influence there expanded even more over the next decade, culminating in his appointment as the company's artistic director in 1986. Levine's role at the Met has been unprecedented in its century-plus history. He has conducted a lion's share of the company's new productions and major revivals while also transforming its orchestra and chorus, now arguably the world's finest. With that success came criticism, but Levine endured and earned much of the credit for his tireless efforts to modernize and popularize the Met and its mission. In his summers off from the Met, he has also led memorable performances at the Salzburg and Bayreuth Festivals. At the same time, Levine has maintained a distinguished career conducting and recording symphonic music with the world's leading orchestras since the 1970s. As a pianist, he also continues to perform chamber music and accompany vocal and instrumental soloists. Under his direction, the Met's orchestra has become an outstanding symphonic ensemble, on the model of the Vienna Philharmonic, and late in 1997 he was named musical director of the Munich Philharmonic. In 2004, he was named Music Director of the famed Boston Symphony. In opera, Levine has been particularly acclaimed for his brilliant, propulsive interpretations of Verdi and Wagner, as well as such 20th-century masterpieces as Berg's *Wozzeck and Lulu* and Schoenberg's *Moses und Aron*.

The Libretto

Act 1

SCENE ONE

A square in Seville.

DISC NO. 1/TRACK 1

Overture. Ta-da! Thus begins one of the most famous of all operatic overtures. Those famous chords are followed by a rising "question-and-answer" sequence that is repeated in the strings and winds, from which the oboe saves a moment of tension by leading the way into a new section where the violins sing a graceful new melody over pizzicato (plucked) low strings (00:53). The dialogue of the opening returns (01:23), with a new element of tension that is confirmed suddenly by forceful chords that echo the overture's opening notes. The atmosphere turns breathlessly urgent (02:01) with a new, melodramatic tune in the minor that seems to sputter angrily, pause to reinforce itself (in the woodwinds) and press on again, exploding finally in a fury (02:31) that spreads throughout the entire orchestra with a fierceness that echoes Beethoven. This "storm" evaporates in the trilling of the violins, carrying the music into the major (03:28) and a suddenly upbeat atmosphere. Over the pulsing of the strings, the oboe pipes a jaunty tune that draws comments from the other winds and the strings. An air of expectation rises from this new mood, with the strings and woodwinds beginning to chatter (04:15) with ever-increasing excitement that finally seems to spend itself. And we are back (04:57) in a sleek restatement of the little musical conflict that was just played. The jaunty little tune returns, with greater brilliance, and it is followed by the chattering of the strings and woodwinds. This time, though, the atmosphere is more exultant. Even the orchestra's crescendo is grander, breaking out at last with a fresh, festive, dance-like melody (06:35) that possesses the entire orchestra. The frenzy grows and grows, mischievously scaling back (07:01) for a brief second, to allow yet another joyous crescendo sweep the overture to its triumphant conclusion.

(To the left is the house with balcony of Don Bartolo. The time is dawn. Fiorello, with a lantern in his hand, introduces various musicians; then Count Almaviva, wrapped up in a mantle.)

Almaviva assembles his serenaders with some marvelous "tip-toe" music and short breathy phrases.

FIORELLO

Piano, pianissimo, senza parlar,

tutti con me venite qua.

FIORELLO

Piano, pianissimo, without a word

all gather around me here.

SUONATORI

Piano, pianissimo, eccoci qua.

MUSICIANS

Piano, pianissimo, here we are.

FIORELLO

Tutto è silenzio, nessun qui sta

che i nostri canti possa turbar.

FIORELLO

All is silence, no one is near

our songs to disturb.

(Count Almaviva, wrapped in a cloak, enters.)

CONTE

Fiorello...Olà!

COUNT

Fiorello...ho!

FIORELLO

Signor, son qua.

FIORELLO

Sir, I am here.

CONTE

Ebben!...gli amici?

COUNT

Well!...and our friends?

FIORELLO

Son pronti già.

FIORELLO

They are all ready.

(He crosses to the musicians.)

CONTE

Bravi, bravissimi, fate silenzio;

piano, pianissimo, senza parlar.

COUNT

Bravi, bravissimi, softly, softly;

piano, pianissimo, utter no word.

SUONATORI	MUSICIANS
Piano, pianissimo, senza parlar.	Piano, pianissimo, without a word.

FIORELLO	FIORELLO
Senza parlar, venite qua.	Without a word, without a word.

CONTE	COUNT
Piano, senza parlar.	Piano, utter no word.

(The musicians tune their instruments, and the Count sings, accompanied by them.)

DISC NO. 1/TRACK 3

Ecco ridente il cielo! The overture's opening chords introduce the accompaniment of the musicians Fiorello has assembled, with woodwinds singing the melody of the Count's serenade over the strumming of the guitar. The Count begins to sing the melody (01:05), beckoning Rosina to come to him. The gentle tune becomes more and more ardent until he thinks he sees her (02:47). The Count erupts into rollicking little expressions of pleasure (in elaborate and decorative phrases called fioritura), echoed in the orchestra. He pauses to wonder at the miracle of love (03:33), before getting carried away once again. He is a man possessed with love, his giddy delight all but bubbling out of him, with his joy carrying him up to an ecstatic high C (04:38).

Ecco ridente in cielo	Lo, in the smiling sky,
spunta la bella aurora,	the lovely dawn is breaking,
e tu non sorgi ancora	and you are not awake,
e puoi dormir così?	and you are still asleep?
Sorgi, mia dolce speme,	Arise, my sweetest love,
vieni bell'idol mio,	oh, come, my treasured one,
rendi men crudo, oh Dio,	soften the pain, O God,
lo stral che mi ferì.	of the dart which pierces me.
Oh sorte! già veggo	Oh, joy! Do I now see
quel caro sembiante,	that dearest vision,
quest'anima amante	has she taken pity
ottenne pietà!	on this soul in love?

Oh, istante d'amore!	Oh, moment of love!
Felice momento!	Oh, moment divine!
Oh, dolce contento	Oh, sweet content
che egual non ha!	which is unequalled!
Ehi, Fiorello?	Ho, Fiorello!

DISC NO. 1/TRACKS 4-6

The musicians enthusiastically thank the Count while he tries to shoo them off in a moment of buoyant silliness.

FIORELLO	**FIORELLO**
Mio signore...	M'lord...
CONTE	**COUNT**
Di', la vedi?	Say, have you seen her?
FIORELLO	**FIORELLO**
Signor no.	No, sir.
CONTE	**COUNT**
Ah, ch'è vana ogni speranza!	Ah, how vain is every hope!
FIORELLO	**FIORELLO**
Signor Conte, il giorno avanza.	Behold, sir, the dawn advances.
CONTE	**COUNT**
Ah, che penso! Che farò?	Ah, what am I to think! what shall I do?
Tutto è vano. Buona gente!	All is vain. Well, my friends!
SUONATORI (*sottovoce*)	**MUSICIANS** (*softly*)
Mio signor...	M'lord...

(The Count is in despair; he dismisses the musicians.)

CONTE	**COUNT**
Avanti, avanti.	Retire, retire.

(He gives a purse to Fiorello, who distributes money to all.)

Più di suoni, più di canti	I have no longer need
io bisogno ormai non ho.	of your songs or your music.

FIORELLO	**FIORELLO**
Buona notte a tutti quanti.	Good night all.
Più di voi che far non so.	I have nothing further for you to do.

(The musicians surround the Count, thanking him and kissing his hand. Annoyed by the noise they make, he tries to drive them away. Fiorello does the same.)

SUONATORI	**MUSICIANS**
Mille grazie, mio signore,	Many thanks, sir, for this favour;
del favore, dell'onore.	better master, nor a braver,
Ah! di tanta cortesia	ever did we sing a stave for.
obbligati in verità!	Pray, good sir, command our throats!
Oh, che incontro fortunato!	We will sing and pray for
È un signore di qualità.	one who gives us gold for notes!

CONTE	**COUNT**
Basta, basta, non parlate,	Silence! Silence! Cease your bawling,
ma non serve, non gridate,	nor, like cats with caterwauling
maledetti, andate via!	wake the neighbours - stop your squalling.
Ah, canaglia, via di qua!	Rascals, get away from here!
Tutto quanto il vicinato	If this noise you still keep making,
questo chiasso sveglierà.	all the neighbours you'll be waking.

FIORELLO	**FIORELLO**
Zitti, zitti, che rumore!	Silence! Silence! What an uproar!
Maledetti, via di qua!	Cursed ones, away from here!
Ve' che chiasso indiavolato,	What a devilish commotion,

ah, che rabbia che mi fa!	I am furious, do you hear!
Maledetti, andate via,	Cursed ones, get out, get out,
ah, canaglia, via di qua!	scoundrels all, away from here!

(Fiorello manages to push the musicians slowly out of the piazza.)

CONTE
Gente indiscreta!

COUNT
Indiscreet rabble!

FIORELLO
Ah, quasi con quel chiasso importuno
tutto quanto il quartiere
han risvegliato.
Alfin sono partiti.

FIORELLO
They had nearly,
with their importunate clamour,
awakened the whole neighbourhood.
At last they're gone!

CONTE *(guardando verso il balcone)*
E non si vede! È inutile sperar.
(Eppur qui voglio aspettar di vederla.
Ogni mattina ella su quel balcone
a prender fresco viene in sull'aurora.
Proviamo.)
Olà, tu ancora ritirati, Fiorel.

COUNT *(looking up at the balcony)*
I can't see her. It's useless to hope.
(Yet I will wait here to glimpse her.
Every morning at dawn she comes out
on that balcony to take the air.
Let's try.)
Ho, there, Fiorello, you can go.

FIORELLO
Vado. Là in fondo attenderò i suoi ordini.

FIORELLO
I'm off. I'll await your orders over there.

(He withdraws.)

CONTE
Con lei se parlar mi riesce,
non voglio testimoni.
Che a quest'ora io tutti i giorni
qui vengo per lei dev'essersi avveduta.
Oh, vedi, amore a un uomo del
mio rango comme l'ha fatta bella!
Eppure, eppure! oh! dev'esser mia sposa.

COUNT
If I manage to talk to her
I don't want witnesses.
She must have noticed that I come
here every day at this time to see her.
Oh, just see what love has done
to a man of my rank!
Yet, yet...oh, she must be my bride...

FIGARO (*dietro le quinte*)

La la la la la la la la la.

FIGARO (*offstage*)

La la la la la la la la la.

CONTE

Chi è mai quest'importuno?

Lasciamolo passar;

sotto quegli archi non veduto

vedrò quanto bisogna.

Già l'alba appare e amor non si vergogna.

COUNT

Who is this coming now?

I'll let him go by;

unseen, under this archway,

I can see what I want.

Dawn is already here but love is not shy.

(He hides, Figaro enters with a guitar around his neck.)

DISC NO. 1/TRACK 7

La ran la le ra...Large al factotum. A vigorous figure in the orchestra announces Figaro's arrival, with the bubbling of the woodwinds serving as his fanfare in this most famous of comic opera arias. Happily singing a stream of nonsense, he is on his way to work. Make way for factotum, he sings happily (00:35), for he is Figaro, a happy man who knows how to ply his trade...and, of course, enjoys the occasional pleasure on the side (01:57). Proudly he enumerates the varied talents for which everyone in Seville—man, woman and child—relies on him. He describes the chaos he encounters on a daily basis, mimicking the cries for assistance he hears all the time. Then, with a hero's bravura (03:57), he recounts how smoothly, surely and quickly he dispatches his many tasks.

FIGARO

La ran la le ra, la ran la la.

Largo al factotum della città!

La ran la la, ecc.

Presto a bottega

che l'alba è già.

La ran la la, ecc.

Ah, che bel vivere,

che bel piacere,

per un barbiere

di qualità.

FIGARO

La ran la le ra, la ran la la.

Make way for the factotum of the city.

La ran la la, etc.

Rushing to his shop

for dawn is here.

La ran la la, etc.

What a merry life,

what gay pleasures

for a barber

of quality.

Ah, bravo Figaro,	Ah, bravo Figaro,
bravo, bravissimo, bravo!	bravo, bravissimo, bravo!
La ran la la, ecc.	La ran la la, etc.
Fortunattisimo	Most fortunate of men,
per verità. Bravo!	indeed you are!
La ran la la, ecc.	La ran la la, etc.
Pronto a far tutto	Ready for everything
la notte, il giorno,	by night or by day,
sempre d'intorno	always in bustle,
in giro sta.	in constant motion.
Miglior cuccagna	A better lot
per un barbiere,	for a barber,
vita più nobile,	a nobler life
no, non si dà.	does not exist.
La la ran la la ran la, ecc.	La la ran la la ran la, etc.
Rasori e pettini,	Razors and combs,
lancette e forbici,	lancets and scissors,
al mio comando	at my command
tutto qui sta.	everything's ready.
V'è la risorsa	Then there are "extras,"
poi del mestiere,	part of my trade,
colla donnetta,	business for ladies
col cavaliere...	and cavaliers...
La la ran la...la...la.	La la ran la...la...la.
Ah, che bel vivere,	Ah, what a merry life,
che bel piacere,	what gay pleasures,
per un barbiere	for a barber
di qualità.	of quality.
Tutti mi chiedono,	All call for me,
tutti mi vogliono,	all want me,
donne, ragazzi,	ladies and children,
vecchi, fanciulle.	old men and maidens.
Qua la parrucca,	I need a wig,
presto la barba,	I want a shave,
qua la sanguigna,	leeches to bleed me,

presto il biglietto.	here, take this note.
Tutti mi chiedono,	All call for me,
tutti mi vogliono.	all want me,
Qua la parrucca,	I need a wig,
presto la barba,	I want a shave,
presto il biglietto.	here, take this note.
Ehi, Figaro, Figaro, Figaro, ecc.	Ho, Figaro, Figaro, Figaro, etc.
Ahimè! Che furia!	Heavens! What a commotion!
Ahimè! che folla!	Heavens! What a crowd!
Uno alla volta,	One at a time,
per carità.	for pity's sake.
Ehi, Figaro; son qua!	Ho, Figaro! I am here!
Figaro qua, Figaro là,	Figaro here, Figaro there,
Figaro su, Figaro giù.	Figaro up, Figaro down.
Pronto, prontissimo	Quicker and quicker
son come il fulmine,	I go like greased lightning,
sono il factotum della città.	make way for the factotum of the city.
Ah, bravo, Figaro,	Ah, bravo, Figaro,
bravo, bravissimo,	bravo, bravissimo,
A te la fortuna	On you good fortune
non mancherà.	will always smile.
La la ran la, ecc.	La la ran la, etc.
Sono il factotum della città.	I am the factotum of the city.

DISC NO. 1/TRACKS 8-12

After his aria, Figaro continues to chatter about himself until interrupted by the Count. They fall silent as Rosina appears on her balcony (track 9) followed by the ever-vigilant Bartolo. Figaro reads aloud (spoken, without music) the letter she drops for the Count, who then begins a lovely and formal serenade to the balcony, accompanied by a guitar (track 11). The serenade is answered by Rosina in the same measured, elegant phrases, until she interrupts herself with a tiny shriek (02:19) as if she were being pulled away from the window. Figaro and the Count return to their conversation in a more animated tone (track 12), each excited by the prospects at hand (love and money).

Ah, che bella vita!	Ah! ah! what a happy life!
Faticar poco, divertirsi assai,	little fatigue, and much amusement,
e in tasca sempre aver	always with some money in my pocket,
qualche doblone,	noble fruition of my reputation.
gran frutto della mia riputazione.	So it is: without Figaro
Ecco qua; senza Figaro	not a girl in Seville can marry;
non si accasa in Siviglia una ragazza;	to me come the little widows
a me la vedovella ricorre pel marito;	for a husband; with the excuse
io, colla scusa del pettine di giorno,	of my comb by day,
della chitarra col favor la notte,	of my guitar by night,
a tutti onestamente, non fo per dir,	to all, and I say it without boasting,
m'adatto a far piacere.	I honestly give service.
Oh, che vita, oh, che mestiere!	Oh, what a life, what a trade!

(Figaro goes up right on the way to his shop; the Count comes out of hiding.)

Orsù, presto a bottega –	Now, away to the shop –

CONTE	**COUNT**
(È desso, oppur m'inganno?)	(It is he, am I mistaken?)

FIGARO	**FIGARO**
(Chi sarà mai costui?)	(Who may this be?)

CONTE	**COUNT**
(Oh, è lui senz'altro!) Figaro...	(Oh! it's certainly he!) Figaro...

FIGARO	**FIGARO**
Mio padrone...Oh! Chi veggo!	My master...oh! Whom do I see?
Eccellenza...	Your Excellency...

CONTE	**COUNT**
Zitto, zitto! Prudenza!	Hush! Be prudent!
Qui non son conosciuto,	I am not known here,
né vo' farmi conoscere.	nor do I wish to be.
Per questo ho le mie gran ragioni.	I have the best of reasons.

FIGARO

Intendo, intendo, la lascio in libertà.

CONTE

No...

FIGARO

Che serve?

CONTE

No, dico, resta qua.
Forse ai disegni miei
non giungi inopportuno.
Ma cospetto! dimmi un po', buona lana,
come ti trovo qua, poter del mondo!
Ti veggo grasso e tondo...

FIGARO

La miseria, signore!

CONTE

Ah, birbo!

FIGARO

Grazie.

CONTE

Hai messo ancor giudizio?

FIGARO

Oh! e come! Ed ella, come in Siviglia?

CONTE

Or te lo spiego. Al Prado
vidi un fior di bellezza, una fanciulla,

FIGARO

I understand, I'll leave you alone.

COUNT

No...

FIGARO

What can I do?

COUNT

No, I tell you, stay here.
Perhaps for my purpose
you've come at the right time.
But tell me, you wily rascal,
how did you come here, Lord Almighty!
I see you're fat and fine...

FIGARO

Hard times brought me, sir!

COUNT

What a scoundrel!

FIGARO

Thank you.

COUNT

Are you behaving yourself?

FIGARO

And how! And you, why in Seville?

COUNT

I will explain. On the Prado
I beheld a flower of beauty, a maiden,

figlia d'un certo medico barbogio
che qua da pochi dì s'è stabilito;
io di questa invaghito,
lasciai patria e parenti;
e qua men venni,
e qui la notte ed il giorno
passo girando a quei balconi intorno.

the daughter of a silly old physician,
who recently established himself here;
enamoured of this damsel,
I left home and country;
and here I came,
and here, night and day,
I watch and wander near this balcony.

FIGARO

A quei balconi? Un medico?
Ah, cospetto! siete ben fortunato;
sui maccheroni, il cacio v'è cascato.

FIGARO

Near this balcony? A physician?
You are very fortunate;
the cheese fell right on the macaroni!

CONTE
Come?

COUNT
Explain!

FIGARO
Certo. Là dentro io son
barbiere, parrucchier, chirurgo.
Botanico, spezial, veterinario...
Insomma, il faccendier di casa.

FIGARO
Certainly. In this house
I am barber, surgeon,
botanist, apothecary, veterinary...
In other words, I run the house.

CONTE
Oh, che sorte!

COUNT
Oh, what luck!

FIGARO
Non basta. La ragazza figlia
non è del medico.
È soltanto la sua pupilla.

FIGARO
But this is not all. The girl is not
the daughter of the physician.
She is only his ward.

CONTE
Oh, che consolazione!

COUNT
Oh, what a consolation!

FIGARO
Perciò...zitto...

FIGARO
But...hush...

CONTE Cos'è?	**COUNT** What is it?
FIGARO S'apre il balcone...	**FIGARO** The balcony window opens...

(Rosina opens the balcony shutters, a piece of paper in her hand.)

ROSINA Non è venuto ancora. Forse...	**ROSINA** He hasn't come yet. Maybe...
CONTE Oh, mia vita! mio nume! mio tesoro! vi veggo alfine, alfine...	**COUNT** Oh, my life! My goddess! My treasure! I see you at last, at last...
ROSINA Oh, che vergogna! vorrei dargli il biglietto...	**ROSINA** Oh, what a shame! I'd like to give him the letter...
BARTOLO *(comparendo sul balcone)* Ebben, ragazza? Il tempo è buono. Cos'è quella carta?	**BARTOLO** *(appearing on the balcony)* Well, girl? The weather's fine. What's that paper?
ROSINA Niente, niente, signore: son le parole dell'aria dell'Inutil precauzione.	**ROSINA** Nothing at all, sir: just the words of the aria from the Futile Precaution.
CONTE Ma brava...dell'Inutil precauzione!	**COUNT** Clever girl...the Futile Precaution?
FIGARO Che furba!	**FIGARO** Crafty minx!

BARTOLO

Cos'è questa Inutil precauzione?

ROSINA

Oh, bella!

è il titolo del nuovo dramma in musica.

BARTOLO

Un dramma! Bella cosa! Sarà al solito un dramma semi-

serio, un lungo, malinconico, noioso,

poetico strambotto.

Barbaro gusto! secolo corrotto!

ROSINA (*lasciando cadere il foglio di carta*)

Oh, me meschina! L'aria m'è caduta.

Raccoglietela presto.

BARTOLO

Vado, vado.

(Bartolo goes inside, Rosina calls to the Count.)

ROSINA

Ps...ps...

CONTE

Ho inteso –

(He picks up the paper.)

ROSINA

Presto.

CONTE

Non temete.

BARTOLO

What is this Futile Precaution?

ROSINA

Well, really!

it's the name of the new opera.

BARTOLO

An opera! Fine thing! As usual it will be a

semi-serious play, a long, melancholy,

boring, poetic rigmarole.

In the worst taste!

What a corrupt age!

ROSINA (*dropping the paper*)

Oh, poor me! it's fallen.

Go and get it at once.

BARTOLO

I'm going, I'm going.

ROSINA

Pst...Pst!

COUNT

I understand –

ROSINA

Quickly.

COUNT

Never fear.

BARTOLO

Son qua. Dov'è?

ROSINA

Ah, il vento l'ha portata via. Guardate.

BARTOLO

Io non la veggo.

Eh, signorina, non vorrei...

(Cospetto! costei m'avesse preso!...)

In casa, in casa, animo, su.

A chi dico? In casa, presto.

ROSINA

Vado, vado. Che furia!

BARTOLO

Quel balcone voglio far murare...

Dentro, dico.

ROSINA

Ah, che vita da crepare!

(Bartolo goes back into the house; Rosina goes inside and closes the balcony shutters.)

CONTE

Povera disgraziata! Il suo stato infelice

sempre più m'interessa.

FIGARO

Presto, presto: vediamo cosa scrive.

CONTE

Appunto. Leggi.

BARTOLO

I'm here. Where is it?

ROSINA

Oh, the wind's blown it away. Look.

BARTOLO

I can't see it.

Now, young lady, I don't want...

(Heavens! she might have tricked me!)...

Go back into the house, be quick about it.

Must I tell you twice? Back into the house,

at once.

ROSINA

I'm going, I'm going. What a fuss!

BARTOLO

I'll have that balcony walled up...

Go inside, I say.

ROSINA

Oh, what an awful life!

COUNT

Poor, unhappy girl! Her sad plight interests

me more and more.

FIGARO

Quickly: let's see what she's written.

COUNT

Exactly. Read it.

(Figaro reads Rosina's letter to the Count.)

FIGARO

"Le vostre assidue premure
hanno eccitata la mia curiosità.
Il mio tutore è per uscir di casa;
appena si sarà allontanato,
procurate con qualche mezzo ingegnoso
d'indicarmi il vostro nome,
il vostro stato e le vostre intenzioni.
Io non posso giammai comparire
al balcone, senza l'indivisibile
compagnia del mio tiranno.
Siate però certo, che tutto è
disposta a fare, per rompere le sue catene,
la sventurata Rosina..."

FIGARO

"Your constant attentions
have aroused my curiosity.
My guardian is just leaving;
as soon as he's gone, find some
ingenious means to tell me your name,
your rank and your intentions.
I can never appear on the balcony
except in the strict company of my tyrant.
Rest assured, however, that
unfortunate Rosina is prepared to do
anything thing to break her
chains."

CONTE

Sì, sì, le romperà.
Su, dimmi un poco:
che razza d'uomo
è questo suo tutore?

COUNT

Yes, yes, she shall break them.
Come, tell me:
what kind of man
is this guardian of hers?

FIGARO

Un vecchio indemoniato,
avaro, sospettoso, brontolone,
avrà cent'anni indosso
e vuol fare il galante:
indovinate!
Per mangiare a Rosina tutta l'eredità
s'è fitto in capo di volerla sposare.
Aiuto!

FIGARO

He's an old devil,
miserly, suspicious, crabbed,
he must be a hundred
but wants to play the gallant:
and just imagine,
so as to enjoy Rosina's entire legacy
he's taken it into his head to marry her.
Help!

CONTE

Che?

COUNT

What is it?

FIGARO

S'apre la porta.

FIGARO

The door's opening.

(The Count and Figaro run away. The door opens and Bartolo comes out of the house.)

BARTOLO

Fra momenti io torno.

Non aprite a nessuno.

Se Don Basilio venisse a ricercarmi,

che m'aspetti.

BARTOLO

I shall return in a few minutes.

Don't let anyone in. If Don Basilio

should come to inquire for me,

let him wait.

(He locks the door from the outside.)

Le mie nozze con lei meglio è affrettare.

I wish to hasten my marriage with her.

(He goes off.)

Sì, dentr'oggi finir vo' quest'affare.

Yes, this day. I am going to conclude this affair.

CONTE

Dentr'oggi le sue nozze con Rosina!

Ah, vecchio rimbambito!

Ma dimmi or tu, chi è questo Don Basilio?

COUNT

This very day, his marriage with Rosina!

Oh, the foolish old dotard!

But tell me, who is this Don Basilio?

FIGARO

È un solenne imbroglion di matrimoni,

un collo torto, un vero disperato,

sempre senza un quattrino...

già, è maestro di musica,

insegna alla ragazza.

FIGARO

A famous, intriguing matchmaker,

a hypocrite, a good-for-nothing,

with never a penny in his pocket...

He has lately turned music-maker,

and teaches this girl.

CONTE

Bene, tutto giova saper.

COUNT

Well, that's good to know.

FIGARO

Ora pensate della bella Rosina
a soddisfar le brame.

CONTE

Il nome mio non le vo' dir
né il grado:
assicurarmi vo' pria ch'ella ami me,
me solo al mondo,
non le ricchezze e i titoli
del Conte Almaviva. Ah! tu potresti...

FIGARO

Io? no, signor;
voi stesso dovete...

CONTE

Io stesso? E come?

FIGARO

Zi...zitto. Eccoci a tiro, osservate:
per bacco, non mi sbaglio.
Dietro la gelosia sta la ragazza:
presto, presto all'assalto, niun ci vede.
In una canzonetta, così alla buona
il tutto spiegatele, signor.

CONTE

Una canzone?

FIGARO

Certo. Ecco la chitarra.
Presto, andiamo.

CONTE

Ma io...

FIGARO

Now you must think how to tell the pretty
Rosina what she wants to know.

COUNT

I don't want to tell her my name
or my rank:
I first want to be sure that she loves me
and me alone in all the world,
not the wealth and titles
of Count Almaviva. Ah, you could...

FIGARO

Me? My lord;
you yourself should...

COUNT

I? But how?

FIGARO

Shhh! What a stroke of luck!
By Jove, I'm not mistaken.
The girl's there behind the shutter.
Quick, quick, into action, no one's looking.
With a simple little song
you can explain it all to her, sir.

COUNT

A song?

FIGARO

Certainly. Here is my guitar.
Come, let's start.

COUNT

But I...

FIGARO

Oh, che pazienza!

CONTE

Ebben, proviamo...
Se il mio nome saper voi bramate,
dal mio labbro il mio nome ascoltate.
Io son Lindoro,
che fido v'adoro,
che sposa vi bramo,
che a nome vi chiamo,
di voi sempre parlando così
dall'aurora al tramonto del dì.

(Rosina answers from behind the shutters.)

ROSINA

Segui, oh caro,
deh, segui così.

FIGARO

Sentite. Ah! che vi pare?

CONTE

Oh, me felice!

FIGARO

Da bravo, a voi, seguite.

CONTE

L'amoroso e sincero Lindoro
non può darvi, mia cara, un tesoro.
Ricco non sono,
ma un core vi dono,
un'anima amante

FIGARO

Heaven give me patience!

COUNT

Well, we'll try...
If you want to know my name,
listen to the song I sing.
I am called Lindoro,
who faithfully adores you,
who wishes to marry you,
your name is on my lips,
and you are in my thoughts,
from early dawn till late at night.

ROSINA

Continue, beloved,
continue to sing.

FIGARO

Listen! What could be better?

COUNT

What happiness!

FIGARO

Bravo! Now continue.

COUNT

Sincere and enamoured Lindoro
cannot give you, my dear, a fortune.
Rich, I am not,
but heart I can give,
a loving spirit

che fida e costante	which faithful and true,
per voi sola sospira, così	for you only breathes,
dall'aurora al tramonto del dì.	from early dawn till late at night.

(Rosina answers again from inside.)

ROSINA

L'amorosa, sincera Rosina	Sincere and enamoured Rosina
del suo core Lindo...	her heart to Lin...

(She breaks off and leaves the balcony.)

CONTE	**COUNT**
Oh, cielo!	Oh, Heavens!

FIGARO	**FIGARO**
Nella stanza convien dir che qualcuno	I imagine someone entered her room.
entrato sia. Ella si è ritirata.	She has gone inside.

CONTE	**COUNT**
Ah, cospettone!	Oh, damnation!
Io già deliro, avvampo!	I am feverish, on fire!
Oh, ad ogni costo	At any cost
vederla io voglio, vo' parlarle!	I must see her, speak to her!
Ah, tu, tu mi devi aiutar.	You, you must help me.

FIGARO	**FIGARO**
Ih, ih, che furia!	Ha, ha, what a frenzy!
Sì, sì, v'aiuterò.	Yes, yes, I shall help you.

CONTE	**COUNT**
Da bravo! Entr'oggi vo' che tu	Bravo! Before nightfall
m'introduca in quella casa.	you must get me into the house.
Dimmi, come farai?	Tell me, how can you do it?
Via, del tuo spirito	Come, let's see some feat
vediam qualche prodezza.	of your imagination.

FIGARO	FIGARO
Del mio spirito!	Of my imagination!
Bene, vedrò...ma in oggi...	Well, I shall see...but nowadays...

CONTE	COUNT
Eh, via! T'intendo.	Yes, yes! I understand.
Va là, non dubitar;	Go ahead, don't worry;
di tue fatiche	your efforts
largo compenso avrai.	will be rewarded.

FIGARO	FIGARO
Davver?	Truly?

CONTE	COUNT
Parola.	On my word.

FIGARO	FIGARO
Dunque oro a discrezione?	Gold in abundance?

CONTE	COUNT
Oro a bizzeffe!	To your heart's content.
Animo, via!	Come, on your way.

DISC NO. 1/TRACK 13

All idea di quel metallo. Figaro and the Count make a plan in the kind of sparkling duet that shows how vividly Rossini explores his characters by repeating, embellishing and contrasting basically simple musical material. Figaro begins earnestly, with a jaunty little tune that bristles with his happy determination to help the Count. A satisfied turn of melody follows (00:48), suggesting that the two are definitely "on the same page" and still thinking. In the exchanges that follow, the two trade off the jaunty tune, with that satisfied-sounding melody suggesting their delight in their plans. But Figaro wonders (3:08): what if the Count played a drunk? He explains (03:43) that Bartolo, perversely, would be more likely to trust a drunk. They agree: what a great idea! (4:22) The two almost part, until the count asks for directions to Figaro's shop. Figaro tells him, in a buoyant waltz-like melody (05:25), where he find the shop; the barber's expression swells with pride. After briefly reassuring each of the terms of the deal, the Count relaunches the waltz melody (06:45), as each of them expresses his own satisfaction and hope in counterpoint to the other. With typically Rossinian punctuation—the excited chattering in the orchestra (07:42)—the Count and Figaro celebrate their cunning.

FIGARO	**FIGARO**
Son pronto. Ah, non sapete	I'm ready. You cannot imagine
i simpatici effetti prodigiosi	what a prodigious devotion
che ad appagare il mio signor Lindoro	the sweet thought of gold
produce in me la dolce idea dell'oro.	makes me feel towards Lindoro.
All'idea di quel metallo	At the idea of this metal
portentoso, onnipossente,	portentous, omnipotent,
un vulcano la mia mente	a volcano within me
già comincia a diventar, sì.	commences to erupt, yes.
CONTE	**COUNT**
Su, vediamo di quel metallo	Come, let's see what effect
qualche effetto sorprendente,	this metal will have on you,
del vulcan della tua mente	some real demonstration
qualche mostro singolar, sì.	of this volcano within you, yes.
FIGARO	**FIGARO**
Voi dovreste travestirvi...	You should disguise yourself...
per esempio...da soldato...	for instance...as a soldier...
CONTE	**COUNT**
Da soldato?	As a soldier?
FIGARO	**FIGARO**
Sì, signore.	Yes, sir.
CONTE	**COUNT**
Da soldato, e che si fa?	As a soldier, and for what purpose?

FIGARO

Oggi arriva un reggimento.

CONTE

Sì, è mio amico il colonello.

FIGARO

Va benon!

CONTE

Eppoi?

FIGARO

Cospetto! Dell'alloggio col biglietto
quella porta s'aprirà.
Che ne dite, mio signore?
Non vi par, non l'ho trovata?
Che invenzione prelibata,
bella, bella in verità!

CONTE

Che invenzione prelibata,
bravo, bravo, in verità!

FIGARO

Piano, piano...un'altra idea!
Veda l'oro cosa fa!
Ubbriaco, mio signor, si fingerà.

CONTE

Ubbriaco?

FIGARO

Sì, signore.

FIGARO

Today a regiment is expected here.

COUNT

Yes, the colonel is a friend of mine.

FIGARO

Excellent!

COUNT

And then?

FIGARO

By means of a billet,
that door will soon open.
What say you to this, sir?
Don't you think I've hit it right?
Isn't it a fine idea,
happy thought, in very truth!

COUNT

Isn't it a fine idea,
happy thought, in very truth!

FIGARO

Softly, softly...another thought!
See the power of your gold!
You must pretend to be drunk.

COUNT

Drunk?

FIGARO

Even so, sir.

CONTE

Ubbriaco? Ma perché?

COUNT

Drunk? But why?

FIGARO

Perché d'un ch'è poco in sé,
che dal vino casca già,
il tutor, credete a me,
il tutor si fiderà.

FIGARO

Because the guardian, believe me,
the guardian would less distrust
a man not quite himself,
but overcome with wine.

ASSIEME

Che invenzione prelibata,
bravo, bravo, in verità!

BOTH

Isn't it a fine idea,
happy thought, in very truth!

CONTE

Dunque?

COUNT

Well, then?

FIGARO

All'opra.

FIGARO

To business.

CONTE

Andiamo.

COUNT

Let's go.

FIGARO

Da bravo.

FIGARO

Bravo.

(They start to leave in opposite directions. The Count calls Figaro back.)

CONTE

Oh, il meglio mi scordavo.
Dimmi un po': la tua bottega,
per trovarti, dove sta?

COUNT

...but the most important thing
I forgot to ask: tell me,
where do I find your shop?

FIGARO

La bottega?...Non si sbaglia...
guardi bene...eccola là...

FIGARO

My shop? you cannot mistake it...
look yonder...there it is...

Numero quindici, a mano manca,
quattro gradini, facciata bianca,
cinque parrucche nella vetrina,
sopra un cartello, "Pomata Fina",
mostra in azzurro alla moderna,
v'è per insegna una lanterna...
Là senza fallo mi troverà.

CONTE

Ho ben capito.

FIGARO

Or vada presto.

CONTE

Tu guarda bene...

FIGARO

Io penso al resto.

CONTE

Di te mi fido...

FIGARO

Colà l'attendo...

CONTE

Mio caro Figaro...

FIGARO

Intendo, intendo...

CONTE

Porterò meco...

number fifteen, on the left hand,
with four steps, a white front,
five wigs in the window,
on a placard, "Pomade Divine",
a show-glass, too, of the latest fashion,
and my sign is a lantern...
There, without fail you will find me.

COUNT

I understand.

FIGARO

You had better go now.

COUNT

And you watch out...

FIGARO

I'll take care of everything.

COUNT

I have faith in you...

FIGARO

I shall wait for you yonder...

COUNT

My dear Figaro...

FIGARO

I understand, I understand...

COUNT

I will bring with me...

FIGARO

La borsa piena.

CONTE

Sì, quel che vuoi,
ma il resto poi...

FIGARO

Oh, non si dubiti,
che bene andrà.

CONTE

Ah, che d'amore
la fiamma io sento,
nunzia di giubilo
e di contento!
D'ardor insolito
quest'alma accende,
e di me stesso
maggior mi fa.
Ah, che d'amore, ecc.
Ecco propizia
che in sen mi scende
d'ardor insolito
quest'alma accende
e di me stesso
maggior mi fa.

FIGARO

Delle monete
il suon già sento,
l'oro già viene...
Eccolo qua.
Già viene l'oro,
viene l'argento,

FIGARO

A purse well filled.

COUNT

Yes, all you want,
but do your part...

FIGARO

Oh, have no doubt,
all will go well.

COUNT

Oh, what a flame
of love divine,
of hope and joy
auspicious sign!
With fire unknown
my soul is burning,
and fills my spirit
with will to dare.
Oh, what a flame, etc.
Oh, glorious moment
which inspires my heart!
With fire unknown
my soul is burning,
and fills my spirit
with will to dare.

FIGARO

I almost can hear
the clinking coin,
gold is coming...
already it's here.
Gold is coming,
silver is coming,

in tasca scende...	filling the pockets...
Eccolo qua.	already it's here.
D'ardore insolito	With fire unknown
quest'alma accende,	my soul is burning,
e di me stesso	and fills my spirit
maggior mi fa.	with will to dare.

(They leave.)

SCENE TWO

A courtyard in Bartolo's house.

DISC NO. 1/TRACK 14

Una voce poco fa. The orchestra almost giggles with delight as it introduces Rosina in this famous and popular solo aria. She sings to herself (00:32), in gently excited little phrases suggesting her delight in being in love. She can barely contain herself when she thinks of Lindoro (01:35), her passion mingling with concern about Bartolo's interference in bursts of coloratura. However, the orchestra informs us as the second part of the aria begins (02:20)...Rosina is not to be underestimated when crossed. She asserts what a sweet girl she is (02:45) until she delivers a very pointed "but" on the Italian word "ma" (03:12). Her ever-bolder flights of coloratura remind us that she has plenty of tricks up her sleeve, as she repeats and emphasizes (in decorated phrases that reach higher and higher) her determination to be with Lindoro.

ROSINA *(con una lettera in mano)*	**ROSINA** *(with a letter in her hand)*
Una voce poco fa	The voice I heard just now
qui nel cor mi risuonò.	has thrilled my very heart.
Il mio cor ferito è già	My heart already is pierced
e Lindoro fu che il piagò.	and it was Lindoro who hurled the dart.
Sì, Lindoro mio sarà,	Yes, Lindoro shall be mine,
lo giurai, la vincerò.	I've sworn it, I'll succeed.

Il tutor ricuserà,	My guardian won't consent,
io l'ingegno aguzzerò,	but I will sharpen my wits,
alla fin s'accheterà,	and at last, he will relent,
e contenta io resterò.	and I shall be content.
Sì, Lindoro ecc.	Yes, Lindoro etc.
Io sono docile,	I am docile,
son rispettosa,	I am respectful,
sono obbediente,	I am obedient,
dolce, amorosa,	sweet and loving.
mi lascio reggere,	I can be ruled,
mi fo guidar.	I can be guided.
Ma se mi toccano	But if crossed in love,
dov'è il mio debole,	I can be a viper,
sarò una vipera, sarò,	and a hundred tricks
e cento trappole	I shall play
prima di cedere farò giocar.	before they have their way.
Io sono docile, ecc.	I am docile, etc.

DISC NO. 1/TRACKS 15-17

Rosina, like Figaro, chatters a bit about herself after her introductory aria (track 15) and then has friendly banter with the equally-spirited Figaro. This is in contrast to the crusty old Bartolo, (track 16) who does not get an aria to announce himself on stage, but merely snarly recitative. His crony, the equally fusty Basilio, is introduced the same way (track 17).

Sì, sì, la vincerò.	Yes, yes, I shall conquer.
Potessi almeno	If I could only
mandargli questa lettera.	send him this letter.
Ma come? Di nessun qui mi fido.	But how? There is none I can trust.
Il tutore ha cent'occhi...	My guardian has a hundred eyes...
Basta...basta...sigilliamola intanto.	Well, well...meanwhile I'll seal it.
Con Figaro, il barbier, dalla finestra	From my window I saw him, for an hour,
discorrer l'ho veduto più d'un'ora.	talking with Figaro, the barber.
Figaro è un galantuomo,	Figaro is an honest fellow,
un giovin di buon core...	a good-hearted soul...

Chi sa ch'ei non protegga
il nostro amore!

who knows, he may be the one
to protect our love!

(Figaro enters from upstage, Rosina hides her letter.)

FIGARO
Oh, buon dì, signorina.

FIGARO
Good day, signorina.

ROSINA
Buon giorno, signor Figaro.

ROSINA
Good day, signor Figaro.

FIGARO
Ebbene? Che si fa?

FIGARO
Well? how are you?

ROSINA
Si muor di noia.

ROSINA
I am dying of boredom.

FIGARO
Oh, diavolo! Possibile!
Una ragazza bella e spiritosa...

FIGARO
The deuce! Is that possible!
A lovely girl, full of spirits...

ROSINA
Ah! Ah! Mi fate ridere!
Che mi serve lo spirito,
che giova la bellezza,
se chiusa sempre sto
fra quattro mura
che mi par d'esser
proprio in sepoltura?

ROSINA
Ah! you make me laugh!
Of what use is my spirit,
what good is my beauty,
if I am always shut up
between four walls
and feel as if I am living
inside a sepulchre?

FIGARO
In sepoltura? Oibò!...
Sentite, io voglio...

FIGARO
A sepulchre? Heavens!...
But I must talk with you...

(The street door is being opened.)

ROSINA

Ecco il tutor.

FIGARO

Davvero?

ROSINA

Certo, certo. È il suo passo.

FIGARO *(ritirandosi)*

Salva, salva! Fra poco ci rivedremo!

Ho da dirvi qualche cosa.

ROSINA

E ancor io, signor Figaro.

FIGARO

Bravissima. Vado.

(He hides himself.)

ROSINA

Quanto è garbato!

(Bartolo enters from the street.)

BARTOLO

Ah, disgraziato Figaro!

Ah, indegno, ah, maledetto,

ah, scellerato!

ROSINA

(Ecco qua. Sempre grida.)

BARTOLO

Ma si può dar di peggio!

ROSINA

My guardian is coming.

FIGARO

Truly?

ROSINA

Definitely. I know his footstep.

FIGARO *(retreating upstage)*

Adieu, adieu! I will see you soon again.

I have something to tell you.

ROSINA

And I too, signor Figaro.

FIGARO

Bravissima. I go.

ROSINA

What a nice fellow he is!

BARTOLO

Oh, that menace of a Figaro!

What a rascal, what a villain,

what a scoundrel!

ROSINA

(He's off again. Always shouting.)

BARTOLO

They don't come any worse!

Un ospedale ha fatto
di tutta la famiglia
a forza d'oppio, sangue e stranutiglia.
Signorina, il barbiere...lo vedeste?

ROSINA
Perché?

BARTOLO
Perché lo vo' sapere!

ROSINA
Forse anch'egli v'adombra?

BARTOLO
E perché no?

ROSINA
Ebben, ve lo dirò.
Sì, l'ho veduto, gli ho parlato,
mi piace, m'è simpatico il suo discorso,
il suo gioviale aspetto.
(Crepa di rabbia, vecchio maledetto!)

(Rosina goes up to her room.)

BARTOLO
Vedete che grazietta!
Più l'amo
e più mi sprezza la briccona.
Certo, certo è il barbiere
che la mette in malizia.
Chi sa cosa le ha detto! Chi sa! Or lo saprò.
Ehi, Berta!
Ambrogio!

With opium, blood and sneezing powder
he has made a hospital
of the whole household.
Signorina, the barber...have you seen him?

ROSINA
Why?

BARTOLO
Why? Because I want to know!

ROSINA
Has he, too, put you in a rage?

BARTOLO
And why not?

ROSINA
Alright, I shall tell you.
Yes, I saw him, I spoke with him,
I like him, I enjoy talking with him,
I find him handsome.
(Choke on that, wicked old man!)

BARTOLO
What a charming little miss!
The more I love her,
the more she disdains me.
There is no doubt, it is the barber
who has put her up to this.
Hey! Berta! Ambrogio! Who knows what
he's told her. I
wonder. Now I'll find out.

(Berta enters, sneezing; Ambrogio also enters, yawning.)

BERTA	**BERTA**
Eccì...	A-tishoo...
AMBROGIO	**AMBROGIO**
Ah ah! Che comanda?	Aah...aah! what are your orders?
BARTOLO	**BARTOLO**
Il barbiere parlato ha con Rosina?	Has the barber been talking to Rosina?
BERTA	**BERTA**
Eccì...	A-tishoo...
BARTOLO	**BARTOLO**
Rispondi almen tu, babbuino.	You answer, at least, you oaf.
AMBROGIO	**AMBROGIO**
Ah ah!	Aah...aah!
BARTOLO	**BARTOLO**
Che pazienza!	Oh, for patience!
AMBROGIO	**AMBROGIO**
Ah ah!...che sonno!	Aah...aah! How sleepy I am!
BARTOLO	**BARTOLO**
Ebben!	Well?
BERTA	**BERTA**
Venne, ma io...	He came, but I...
BARTOLO	**BARTOLO**
Rosina...?	And Rosina...?

AMBROGIO

Ah ah!

BERTA

Eccì...

BARTOLO

Che serve! eccoli qua, son mezzo morti.
Andate.

AMBROGIO

Ah ah!

BERTA

Eccì...

BARTOLO

Eh, il diavolo che vi porti!
Ah! Barbiere d'inferno...
Tu me la pagherai!

(chases both of them away. Basilio enters.)

Qua, Don Basilio, giungete a tempo.
Oh! io voglio per forza o per amor
dentro dimani sposar la mia Rosina.
Avete inteso?

DON BASILIO

Eh, voi dite benissimo,
e appunto io qui veniva ad avvisarvi.
Ma segretezza...
È giunto il Conte Almaviva.

BARTOLO

Chi? L'incognito amante della Rosina?

AMBROGIO

Aah...aah!

BERTA

A-tishoo...

BARTOLO

What servants! Here they are, half dead.
Go now!

AMBROGIO

Aah...aah!

BERTA

A-tishoo...

BARTOLO

Oh, the devil take the pair of you!
Oh! Devil of a barber...
You shall pay for this!

Don Basilo, you come at the right time.
By force or by love,
by tomorrow I must marry Rosina.
Is that clear?

DON BASILIO

Eh, you speak wisely,
and it is for that very reason I have come.
But keep this secret...
Count Almaviva has arrived.

BARTOLO

Who? The unknown lover of Rosina?

DON BASILIO

Appunto quello.

BARTOLO

Oh, diavolo! Ah! Qui ci vuol rimedio.

DON BASILIO

Certo. Ma alla sordina.

BARTOLO

Sarebbe a dir?

DON BASILIO

Così, con buona grazia,
bisogna principiare
a inventar qualche favola
che al pubblico lo metta in mala vista,
che comparir lo faccia
un uomo infame, un'anima perduta...
Io, io vi servirò;
fra quattro giorni, credete a me,
Basilio ve lo giura,
noi lo farem sloggiar
da queste mura.

BARTOLO

E voi credete?

DON BASILIO

Oh, certo! È il mio sistema,
e non sbaglia.

BARTOLO

E vorreste? Ma...una calunnia...

DON BASILIO

The very same.

BARTOLO

Oh, the devil! Something must be done.

DON BASILIO

Certainly. But very hush-hush.

BARTOLO

That is to say?

DON BASILIO

Just this, that plausibly,
we must begin
to invent a story
which will put him in a bad light
with the public, making him seem
a man of infamy, a doomed soul...
I shall attend to this;
within four days,
on the word of Basilio,
he'll be thrown out
of this town.

BARTOLO

Do you really think so?

DON BASILIO

Without a doubt! I have my own system,
and it is foolproof.

BARTOLO

And you would dare? But...calumny...

DON BASILIO

Ah, dunque la calunnia cos'è!

Voi non sapete?

DON BASILIO

Ah, what is calumny!

Don't you know?

BARTOLO

No, davvero.

BARTOLO

In truth, I do not.

DISC NO. 1/TRACK 18

La calunnia è un venticello. A stately melody announces Don Basilio's sermon-like explanation of calumny and its infectious nature. This aria is one of the staples of the bass repertory and a superb example of the power of Rossini's techniques for illustrating a character with subtleties and musical innuendo. Accompanied by the kind of "busy" Rossini musical figure that should be familiar by now (00:56), he describes the way it spreads, with the music swelling and intensifying—another trademark Rossini crescendo—into an explosion. Catching his breath after this outburst (02:40), a new melody allows Basilio to smugly make (and reinforce) his point: calumny can kill a poor soul.

DON BASILIO

No? Uditemi e tacete.

La calunnia è un venticello

un'auretta assai gentile

che insensibile, sottile,

leggermente, dolcemente,

incomincia a sussurrar.

Piano, piano, terra terra,

sottovoce, sibilando,

va scorrendo, va ronzando.

Nell'orecchie della gente,

s'introduce destramente

e le teste ed i cervelli

fa stordire e fa gonfiar.

Dalla bocca fuori uscendo

lo schiamazzo va crescendo,

prende forza a poco a poco,

DON BASILIO

No? Then hear and be silent.

Calumny is a little breeze,

a gentle zephyr

which insensibly, subtly,

lightly and sweetly,

commences to whisper.

Softly, softly, here and there,

sottovoce, sibilant,

it goes gliding, it goes rambling.

In the ears of the people,

it penetrates slyly

and the head and the brains

it stuns and it swells.

From the mouth re-emerging

the noise grows crescendo,

gathers force little by little,

vola già di loco in loco,	runs its course from place to place,
sembra il tuono, la tempesta	seems like the thunder of the tempest
che nel sen della foresta	which from the depths of the forest
va fischiando, brontolando,	comes whistling, muttering,
e ti fa d'orror gelar.	freezing everyone in horror.
Alla fin trabocca e scoppia,	Finally with crack and crash,
si propaga, si raddoppia,	it spreads afield, its force redoubled,
e produce un'esplosione	and produces an explosion
come un colpo di cannone,	like the outburst of a cannon,
un tremuoto, un temporale,	an earthquake, a whirlwind,
che fa l'aria rimbombar.	which makes the air resound.
E il meschino calunniato,	And the poor slandered wretch,
avvilito, calpestato,	vilified, trampled down,
sotto il pubblico flagello,	sunk beneath the public lash,
per gran sorte va a crepar.	by good fortune, falls to death.
Ah! Che ne dite?	Now what do you say?

DISC NO. 1/TRACKS 19-20

The old men's fussing and plotting is again contrasted with the bouncier repartee of Rosina and Figaro (track 20), brimming with youthful confidence.

BARTOLO	**BARTOLO**
Eh! Sarà ver, ma intanto si perde tempo	Eh! that may be true, but meanwhile
e qui stringe il bisogno.	we are wasting valuable time.
No, vo' fare a modo mio.	No, I want to do things my own way.
In mia camera andiam.	Let's go into my room.
Voglio che insieme il contratto di nozze	Together the marriage contract
ora stendiamo. Quando sarà mia moglie,	we must prepare. When she is my wife,
(moving off to his room)	I shall know very well
da questi zerbinotti innamorati	how to keep off these lovestick dandies.
metterla in salvo sarà pensier mio.	

DON BASILIO (seguendolo)	**DON BASILIO** (following him)
(Vengan denari,	(If there is money to make,
al resto son qua io.)	I am always on hand.)

(Figaro, who has been hiding, comes forward.)

FIGARO

Ma bravi! Ma benone! Ho inteso tutto.
Evviva il buon Dottore! Povero babbuino!
Tua sposa? Eh, via!
Pulisciti il bocchino!
Or che stanno là chiusi
procuriam di parlare alla ragazza...

(Rosina comes down from her room.)

Eccola appunto.

ROSINA

Ebbene, signor Figaro?

FIGARO

Gran cose, signorina.

ROSINA

Sì, davvero?

FIGARO

Mangerem dei confetti.

ROSINA

Come sarebbe a dir?

FIGARO

Sarebbe a dire
che il vostro bel tutore ha stabilito
esser dentro doman vostro marito.

ROSINA

Eh, via!

FIGARO

Bravo! all goes well! I heard everything.
Hurrah for the good Doctor! Poor idiot!
Your wife? Come, come!
Don't make me laugh!
While they are shut up in that room
I shall try to talk to the girl...

But here she is.

ROSINA

Well, signor Figaro?

FIGARO

Great things are happening, signorina.

ROSINA

Indeed?

FIGARO

We shall eat wedding-cake soon.

ROSINA

What do you mean?

FIGARO

I mean to say
that this fine guardian of yours
plans to be your husband by tomorrow.

ROSINA

What nonsense!

FIGARO

Oh, ve lo giuro.

A stender il contratto

col maestro di musica

là dentro s'è serrato.

ROSINA

Sì? Oh, l'ha sbagliata affè!

Povero sciocco!

L'avrà da far con me...

Ma dite, signor Figaro,

voi poco fa sotto le mie finestre

parlavate a un signore?

FIGARO

(moving away from Rosina, and making up a story)

Ah, un mio cugino.

Un bravo giovinotto,

buona testa, ottimo cor.

Qui venne i suoi studi a compire

e il poverin cerca di far fortuna.

ROSINA

Fortuna? Eh, la farà.

FIGARO

Oh, ne dubito assai.

In confidenza, ha un gran difetto addosso.

ROSINA

Un gran difetto?

FIGARO

Ah, grande. È innamorato morto.

FIGARO

Oh, I swear it.

He has locked himself

in that room with your music-master

to draw up the contract.

ROSINA

Yes? Well, he is much mistaken!

Poor fool!

He has me to deal with...

but tell me, signor Figaro,

a little while ago under my window

were you talking with a gentleman?

FIGARO

Yes, with my cousin.

A fine young man,

with a good head and a warm heart.

Poor fellow, he has come here

to finish his studies and to seek his fortune.

ROSINA

A fortune? Oh, he'll make it.

FIGARO

I doubt it.

Confidentially he has one great fault.

ROSINA

A great fault?

FIGARO

Yes, a great one. He is dying of love.

ROSINA

Sì, davvero? Quel giovine, vedete,
m'interessa moltissimo.

FIGARO

Per bacco!

ROSINA

Non ci credete?

FIGARO

Oh, sì!

ROSINA

E la sua bella, dite,
abita lontano?

FIGARO

Oh, no! Cioè...qui...due passi...

ROSINA

Ma è bella?

FIGARO

Oh, bella assai!
Eccovi il suo ritratto in due parole:
grassotta, genialotta,
capello nero, guancia porporina,
occhio che parla, mano che innamora.

ROSINA

E il nome?

FIGARO

Ah, il nome ancora! Il nome,
che bel nome! Si chiama...

ROSINA

Really? That young man, you know,
interests me very much.

FIGARO

Good Lord!

ROSINA

Don't you believe it?

FIGARO

Oh, yes!

ROSINA

And tell me, his beloved,
does she live far away?

FIGARO

Oh, no! That is...here...two steps...

ROSINA

But is she pretty?

FIGARO

Oh, pretty enough!
I can give you her picture in two words:
deliciously plump, high-spirited,
black hair, rosy cheeks,
sparkling eyes, enchanting hands.

ROSINA

And her name?

FIGARO

And her name too! Her name,
what a lovely name! She is called...

ROSINA	**ROSINA**
Ebben? Si chiama?	Well, what is she called?
FIGARO	**FIGARO**
Poverina!...	Poor little dear!...
Si chiama R...O...Ro...	She is called R...O...Ro...
S...I...si...Rosi...	S...I...si...Rosi...
FIGARO E ROSINA	**FIGARO AND ROSINA**
N...A...na...	...N...A...na...
Rosina!	Rosina!

Dunque io son. Learning that she is indeed the beloved of Lindoro, Rosina stutters her delight, though volleys of coloratura give her away: she already knows. Figaro responds (00:46), in wry echoes of the melody and coloratura Rosina has just sung. The conversational exhanges that follow show Rossini's gift for writing witty musical chitchat. The melodic material is varied only slightly, often in the musical elaborations that reflect the point being made in the text. Their excitement bubbles up in another Rossini crescendo (03:38), which (also typically) pulls back with a second thought, before hurtling to a brilliant conclusion.

ROSINA	**ROSINA**
Dunque io son...tu non m'inganni?	Then it is I...You are not mocking me?
Dunque io son la fortunata!	Then I am the fortunate girl!
(Già me l'ero immaginata,	(But I had already guessed it,
lo sapevo pria di te.)	I knew it all along.)
FIGARO	**FIGARO**
Di Lindoro il vago oggetto	You are, sweet Rosina,
siete voi, bella Rosina.	of Lindoro's love, the object.
(Oh, che volpe sopraffina!	(Oh, what a cunning little fox!
Ma l'avrà da far con me.)	But she'll have to deal with me.)

ROSINA

Senti, senti, ma a Lindoro
per parlar come si fa?

FIGARO

Zitto, zitto, qui Lindoro
per parlarvi ora sarà.

ROSINA

Per parlarmi? Bravo! Bravo!
Venga pur, ma con prudenza,
io già moro d'impazienza!
Ma che tarda? Cosa fa?

FIGARO

Egli attende qualche segno,
poverin, del vostro affetto;
sol due righe di biglietto
gli mandate e qui verrà.
Che ne dite?

ROSINA

Non vorrei...

FIGARO

Su, coraggio.

ROSINA

Non saprei...

FIGARO

Sol due righe...

ROSINA

Mi vergogno.

ROSINA

But tell me, to Lindoro
how shall I contrive to speak?

FIGARO

Patience, patience, and Lindoro
soon your presence here will seek.

ROSINA

To speak to me? Bravo! Bravo!
Let him come, but with caution,
meanwhile I am dying of impatience!
Why is he delayed? What is he doing?

FIGARO

He is awaiting some sign,
poor man, of your affection;
send him but two lines
and you will see him here.
What do you say to this?

ROSINA

I shouldn't...

FIGARO

Come, courage.

ROSINA

I don't know...

FIGARO

Only two lines...

ROSINA

I am too shy.

FIGARO

Ma di che? Ma di che? Si sa!
Presto, presto, qua il biglietto.

ROSINA

Un biglietto?...Eccolo qua.

(She takes a letter from her bosom and gives it to him.)

FIGARO

(Già era scritto...Ve' che bestia!
Il maestro faccio a lei!)

ROSINA

Fortunati affetti miei,
io comincio a respirar.

FIGARO

(Ah, che in cattedra costei
di malizia può dettar.)

ROSINA

Ah, tu solo, amor, tu sei
che mi devi consolar.

FIGARO

(Donne, donne, eterni dei,
chi v'arriva a indovinar?)

ROSINA

Ah, tu solo, amor, tu sei
che mi devi consolar.

ROSINA

Senti, senti, ma Lindoro...

FIGARO

But why? But why?
Quickly, quickly, give me a note.

ROSINA

A note?...Here it is.

FIGARO

(Already written...what a fool!
She could give me a lesson or two!)

ROSINA

Fortunate smiles on my love,
I can breathe once more.

FIGARO

(In cunning itself
she could be a professor.)

ROSINA

Oh, you alone, my love,
can console my heart.

FIGARO

(Women, women, eternal gods,
who can fathom their minds?)

ROSINA

Oh, you alone, my love,
can console my heart.

ROSINA

Tell me, but Lindoro...

FIGARO

Qui verrà.

A momenti per parlarvi qui sarà.

FIGARO

Is on his way. In a few minutes

he'll be here to speak to you.

ROSINA

Venga pur, ma con prudenza.

ROSINA

Let him come, but with caution.

FIGARO

Zitto, zitto, qui verrà.

FIGARO

Patience, patience, he'll be here.

ROSINA

Fortunati affetti miei,

io comincio a respirar.

Ah, tu solo, amor, tu sei,

che mi devi consolar.

ROSINA

Fortune smiles on my love,

I can breathe once more.

Oh, you alone, my love,

can console my heart.

FIGARO

(Donne, donne, eterni dei,

chi v'arriva a indovinar?)

FIGARO

(Women, women, eternal gods,

who can fathom their minds?)

(Figaro leaves through the street door.)

ROSINA

Ora mi sento meglio,

questo Figaro è un bravo giovinotto.

ROSINA

Now I feel better.

That Figaro is a nice young man.

(Bartolo enters from his room.)

BARTOLO

Insomma, colle buone

potrei sapere dalla mia Rosina

che venne a far colui questa mattina?

BARTOLO

With fair words may I know

from my Rosina what brought

this fellow here this morning?

ROSINA

Figaro? Non so nulla.

ROSINA

Figaro? I know nothing.

BARTOLO

Ti parlò?

BARTOLO

He spoke to you?

ROSINA

Mi parlò.

ROSINA

He spoke to me.

BARTOLO

Che ti diceva?

BARTOLO

What was he telling you?

ROSINA

Oh, mi parlò di certe bagatelle...
Dei figurin di Francia,
del mal della sua figlia Marcellina.

ROSINA

Oh, he told me a hundred trifles...
Of the fashions in France,
of the illness of his daughter, Marcellina.

BARTOLO

Davvero?
Ed io scommetto...
che portò
la risposta al tuo biglietto.

BARTOLO

Indeed?
And I wager...
...that he brought
the reply to your note.

ROSINA

Qual biglietto?

ROSINA

What note?

BARTOLO

Che serve!
L'arietta dell'Inutil precauzione
che ti cadde staman giù
dal balcone.
Vi fate rossa?
(Avessi indovinato!)
Che vuol dir questo dito
così sporco d'inchiostro?

BARTOLO

Oh, what's the use?
The air from The Futile Precaution
which you dropped this morning
from the balcony.
You're blushing, eh?
(If only I'd guessed!)
What is the meaning
of your ink-stained finger?

ROSINA

Sporco? Oh! Nulla.

ROSINA

Stained? Oh! nothing.

Io me l'avea scottato
e coll'inchiostro
or l'ho medicato.

BARTOLO
(Diavolo!)
E questi fogli...
or son cinque, eran sei.

ROSINA
Que' fogli? È vero.
D'uno mi son servita a mandar
de' confetti a Marcellina.

BARTOLO
Bravissima!
E la penna
perché fu temperata?

ROSINA
(Maledetto!) La penna!
Per disegnare un fiore sul tamburo.

BARTOLO
Un fiore!

ROSINA
Un fiore.

BARTOLO
Un fiore! Ah! Fraschetta!

ROSINA
Davver.

I burned myself
and I used the ink
as a medicine.

BARTOLO
The devil!
And these sheets of paper...
there are five now, there were six.

ROSINA
The note paper? You are right.
I used one to wrap the sweets
I sent to Marcellina.

BARTOLO
Bravissima!
And the pen,
why was it sharpened?

ROSINA
(Heavens!) The pen!
To draw a flower to embroider.

BARTOLO
A flower!

ROSINA
A flower.

BARTOLO
A flower! Oh! you minx!

ROSINA
It is the truth.

BARTOLO	BARTOLO
Zitto.	Silence.

ROSINA	ROSINA
Credete...	Believe me...

BARTOLO	BARTOLO
Basta così.	Enough of this.

ROSINA	ROSINA
Signor...	Sir...

DISC NO. 1/TRACKS 22 & 23

A un dottor della mia sorte. Rosina's interrogation by Basilio is full of short, clipped phrases that go nowhere, typical of her uncomfortable relationship with him and in contrast to her bubbling exchanges with the friendly Figaro. The doctor then gives vent to his feelings (track 23) in his long narrative aria, a gem of the Italian comic tradition for the bass voice (basso buffo). It is as notoriously challenging for the singer as it is delightful for the audience. Bartolo begins describing his own "virtues" in almost heroic terms (note the "Ta-da" figures in the orchestra at 01:05, more appropriate for a warrior than a dirty old man). He repeats himself and works himself into a lather, breaking into a patter (03:19) that is among the fastest (and funniest) a bass is ever required to sing. After almost giving himself a fit (written into the music at 04:05), Bartolo repeats where he began, giving us the impression that these paroxysms of his are typical occurrences and perhaps even a bit rehearsed.

BARTOLO	BARTOLO
Non più...tacete.	No more...be quiet.
A un dottor della mia sorte	For a doctor of my standing
queste scuse, signorina,	these excuses, signorina,
vi consiglio, mia carina,	I advise you, my dear child,
un po' meglio a impostar.	to invent a little better.
Meglio! Meglio! Meglio! Meglio!	Better! Better! Better! Better!
I confetti alla ragazza!	Sweets for Marcellina!
Il ricamo sul tamburo!	A design for your embroidery!

Vi scottaste, eh via!
Ci vuol altro, figlia mia,
per potermi corbellar.
Altro! Altro! Altro! Altro!
Perché manca là quel foglio?
Vo' saper cotesto imbroglio.
Sono inutili le smorfie;
ferma là, non mi toccate.
Figlia mia, non lo sperate
ch'io mi lasci infinocchiar.
A un dottor della mia sorte
queste scuse, signorina,
vi consiglio, mia carina,
un po' meglio a imposturar.
Via carina, confessate.
Son disposto a perdonar.
Non parlate? Vi ostinate?
So ben io quel che ho da far.
Signorina, un'altra volta
quando Bartolo andrà fuori
la consegna ai servitori
a suo modo far saprà.
Eh! non servono le smorfie,
faccia pur la gatta morta.
Cospetton! per quella porta,
nemmen l'aria entrar potrà,
e Rosina innocentina,
sconsolata, disperata,
eh! non servono le smorfie,
faccia pur la gatta morta.
Cospetton! per quella porta
nemmen l'aria entrar potrà.
E Rosina innocentina,
sconsolata, disperata,
in sua camera serrata,

And the scalding of your finger!
It takes more than that, my girl,
to deceive me successfully.
More! More! More! More!
Why is that sheet of paper missing?
I mean to find out what's going on.
It's no use pulling faces.
Stop, don't touch me.
No, my dear girl, give up all hope
that I'll let myself be fooled.
For a doctor of my standing
these excuses, signorina,
I advise you my dear child,
to invent a little better.
Come, dear child, confess it all.
I am prepared to pardon you.
You don't answer? You are stubborn?
Then I know well what I'll do.
Signorina, another time
when Bartolo must leave the house,
he'll give orders to the servants
who will see you stay inside.
Now your pouting will not help you
nor your injured innocence.
I here assure you, through that door
the very air itself won't enter.
And little innocent Rosina,
disconsolate and in despair,
now your pouting will not help you,
nor your injured innocence.
I here assure you, through that door
the very air itself won't enter,
and little innocent Rosina,
disconsolate and in despair,
in her chamber shall be locked

fin ch'io voglio star dovrà.	so long as I see fit.
Sì, sì, sì, sì, ecc.	Yes, yes, yes, yes, etc.
Un dottor della mia sorte	For a doctor of my standing
non si lascia infinocchiar,	does not let himself be fooled.
e Rosina innocentina, ecc.	And little innocent Rosina, etc.

(They exit. Berta enters.)

DISC NO. 2/TRACKS 1 & 2

The ever-sneezing Berta lets in the (supposedly) drunk Count Almaviva, who in addition to being generally obnoxious, has some fun with Bartolo's name ("Balordo" means "stammer").

BERTA	**BERTA**
Finora in questa camera	From within this room
mi parve di sentir un mormorio...	I thought I heard a noise...
Sarà stato il tutor colla pupilla...	Probably the guardian with his ward...
non ha un'ora di ben.	He never has an hour's peace.
Queste ragazze non la voglion capir...	These girls don't want to understand...

(She hears a knock and the voice of the Count outside.)

Battono!	Knocking!

CONTE	**COUNT**
Aprite.	Open.

BERTA	**BERTA**

(going to open the street door)

Vengo...Eccì...ancora dura:	I am coming...A-tishoo..., it keeps on and
quel tobacco m'ha posto in sepoltura!	on. That snuff has done for me!

(She opens the door. The Count enters disguised as a soldier. He pretends to be drunk. Berta goes out and Bartolo enters.)

CONTE

Ehi, di casa, buona gente...

niun risponde! Ehi...

BARTOLO

Chi è costui? Che brutta faccia!

È ubbriaco! Chi sarà?

CONTE

Ehi, di casa, maledetti! Ehi...

BARTOLO

Cosa vuol, signor soldato?

CONTE

Ah, sì!

Bene obbligato.

BARTOLO

(Qui costui che mai vorrà?)

CONTE

Siete voi...aspetta un poco...

Siete voi...dottor Balordo?

BARTOLO

Che Balordo? Che Balordo?

CONTE

Ah, ah, Bertoldo?

BARTOLO

Che Bertoldo? Eh, andate al diavolo!

Dottor Bartolo, Dottor Bartolo.

COUNT

Hey, good people...

Is no one at home! Hey...

BARTOLO

Who can that be? What an ugly face!

And drunk, too! Who is it?

COUNT

Curses, is nobody home! Hey...

BARTOLO

What do you want, signor Soldier?

COUNT

Oh, yes!

Very much obliged.

BARTOLO

(What on earth is he doing here?)

COUNT

You are...wait a minute...

You are...Doctor Balordo?

BARTOLO

What Balordo? What Balordo?

COUNT

Ah, ah, Bertoldo?

BARTOLO

What Bertoldo? Oh, go to the devil!

Doctor Bartolo, Doctor Bartolo.

CONTE
Ah, bravissimo;
Dottor Barbaro; bravissimo,
Dottor Barbaro.

BARTOLO
Un corno!

CONTE
Va benissimo,
già v'è poca differenza.

BARTOLO *(trascinandosi, infuriato)*
(Io già perdo la pazienza.
Qui prudenza ci vorrà.)

CONTE *(in cerca di Rosina)*
(Non si vede! Che impazienza!
Quanto tarda! Dove sta?)
Dunque voi siete dottore?

BARTOLO
Son dottore, sì, signore.

CONTE
Va, benissimo! Un abbraccio,
qua, collega.

BARTOLO
Indietro!

CONTE
Qua. Sono anch'io
dottor per cento...
Maniscalco al reggimento.

COUNT
Ah, bravissimo,
Doctor Barbaro, bravissimo,
Doctor Barbaro.

BARTOLO
You blockhead!

COUNT
Well and good,
the difference, after all, is trifling.

BARTOLO *(shuffling, in a fury)*
(I am already out of patience.
Prudence is necessary here.)

COUNT *(searching for Rosina)*
(She does not appear! How impatient I
feel! How long she delays! Where can she
be?) Then you are a doctor?

BARTOLO
Yes, sir, I am a doctor.

COUNT
Ah, very fine! Let me embrace
a colleague here.

BARTOLO
Keep off!

COUNT
Come. I also am
a qualified doctor,
I am the vet of the regiment.

Dell'alloggio sul biglietto
osservate, eccolo qua.
(Ah, venisse, il caro oggetto
della mia felicità!)

BARTOLO
(Dalla rabbia, dal dispetto
io già crepo in verità.
Ah, ch'io fo, se mi ci metto,
qualche gran bestialità.)

(Rosina enters from her room.)

CONTE
Vieni, vieni, il tuo diletto,
pien d'amor t'attende già.

BARTOLO
Ah, ch'io fo, se mi ci metto,
qualche gran bestialità!

ROSINA
(Un soldato, il tutore,
cosa mai faranno qua?)

(The Count has seen Rosina and approaches her.)

CONTE
(È Rosina! Or son contento.)

ROSINA
(Ei mi guarda...s'avvicina.)

CONTE
(Son Lindoro!)

My billet for lodgings,
look, here it is.
(Oh, come, dearest object
of my happiness!)

BARTOLO
(With rage, with vexation
in truth I shall burst.
If I don't watch out,
I'll do something rash.)

COUNT
Hasten, hasten, your adorer,
full of love, awaits you here.

BARTOLO
If I don't watch out,
I'll do something rash.

ROSINA
(A soldier, my guardian,
what am I to do now?)

COUNT
(It is Rosina! Now I am happy.)

ROSINA
(He looks at me...he is coming near.)

COUNT
(I am Lindoro!)

ROSINA

(Oh, ciel! Che sento! Ah, giudizio,
ah, giudizio, per pietà!)

BARTOLO *(vedendo Rosina)*

Signorina, che cercate?
Presto, presto, andate via!

ROSINA

Vado, vado, non gridate.

BARTOLO

Presto, presto, via di qua.

CONTE

Ehi, ragazza, vengo anch'io.

BARTOLO

Dove, dove, signor mio?

CONTE

In caserma.

BARTOLO

In caserma?

CONTE

Oh, questa è bella!

BARTOLO

In caserma?
Bagatella!

CONTE

Cara...

ROSINA

(Heavens! What do I hear!
Prudence, for mercy's sake!)

BARTOLO *(seeing Rosina)*

Signorina, what are you looking for?
Quickly, quickly, leave the room!

ROSINA

I'm going, I'm going, don't shout.

BARTOLO

Quickly, quickly, away from here.

COUNT

And, my girl, I am going too.

BARTOLO

Where, where, sir?

COUNT

To the barracks.

BARTOLO

To the barracks?

COUNT

Oh, this is great!

BARTOLO

To the barracks?
A good joke!

COUNT

Dearest...

ROSINA

Aiuto...

ROSINA

Help me...

BARTOLO

Olà, cospetto!

BARTOLO

Oh, damnation!

CONTE

Dunque vado...

COUNT

Then I go...

(The Count starts toward the inner room. Bartolo seizes him.)

BARTOLO

Oh, no signore,

qui d'alloggio non può star.

BARTOLO

Oh, no, sir,

you can have no lodging here.

CONTE

Come? Come?

COUNT

What? What?

BARTOLO

Eh, non v'è replica...

Ho il brevetto d'esenzione.

BARTOLO

No sense arguing...

I am exempt from lodging troops.

CONTE

Il brevetto?

COUNT

Exempt?

BARTOLO *(andando allo scrittoio)*

Mio padrone, un momento

e il mostrerò.

BARTOLO *(going to his desk)*

Good sir, just a moment

and I shall show you.

CONTE *(piano a Rosina)*

Ah, se qui restar non posso,

deh, prendete...

COUNT *(aside to Rosina)*

Since I may not be able to remain here,

take this...

(He motions to her to take a note.)

ROSINA	**ROSINA**
(Ohimè! Ci guarda!)	(Be careful! He is watching us!)
BARTOLO	**BARTOLO**
(Ah, trovarlo ancor non posso.)	(Oh, I can no longer find it.)
ROSINA	**ROSINA**
(Prudenza!)	(We must be careful!)
BARTOLO	**BARTOLO**
(Ma, sì, sì, lo troverò.)	(But, yes, yes, I must find it.)
ROSINA E CONTE	**ROSINA AND COUNT**
(Cento smanie io sento addosso,	(A hundred emotions burn within me,
ah, più reggere non so.)	I can no longer control myself.)
BARTOLO	**BARTOLO**
Ah, ecco qua.	Ah, here it is.

(He comes forward with a document in his hand and reads.)

"Con la presente il Dottor Bartolo,	"By this let it be known
eccetera, esentiamo..."	that Doctor Bartolo etc. is exempted..."
CONTE *(con un rovescio di mano manda*	**COUNT** *(with a sweep of his hand, flings the*
in aria la pergamena)	*paper into the air)*
Eh, andate al diavolo!	Oh, go to the devil!
Non mi state più a seccar.	Don't bother me any more.
BARTOLO	**BARTOLO**
Cosa fa, signor mio caro?	My dear sir, what are you doing?
CONTE *(andando verso Rosina)*	**COUNT** *(crossing right to Rosina)*
Zitto là, dottor somaro;	Silence now, donkey of a doctor;
il mio alloggio è qui fissato,	my lodging is fixed here,
e in alloggio qui vo' star.	and here I will remain.

BARTOLO

Vuol restar?

CONTE

Restar, sicuro.

BARTOLO

(thrashing the Count with his walking stick)

Oh, son stufo, mio padrone,
presto fuori, o un buon bastone
lo farà di qua sloggiar!

CONTE

Dunque, lei vuol battaglia?
Ben! Battaglia le vo' dar.

(drawing his sword)

Bella cosa è una battaglia!
Ve la voglio qui mostrar.

(He knocks the stick out of Bartolo's hand.)

Osservate! Questo è il fosso...
L'inimico voi sarete...
Attenzion, e gli amici...

(aside to Rosina)

(Giù il fazzoletto.)

(He lets a letter fall and Rosina drops her handkerchief to cover it.)

BARTOLO

Will remain?

COUNT

Certainly, will remain.

BARTOLO

I am fed up, my master,
out and quickly, or a good stick
will dislodge you from here!

COUNT

Then you wish to battle?
Good! A battle I will give you.

A battle is a fine thing!
Let me show you how it's done.

Observe! This is the trench...
You are the enemy...
Attention, and my friends...

(Drop your handkerchief.)

E gli amici, stan di qua, attenzion.

BARTOLO

(who has noticed the manoeuvre)

Ferma, ferma...

CONTE
Che cos'è? Ah!

BARTOLO
Vo' vedere.

(As Bartolo bends to pick up the letter, the Count puts his sword through it.)

CONTE
Sì, se fosse una ricetta!...
Ma un biglietto...È mio dovere...
Mi dovete perdonar.

(He gives the note to Rosina who quickly exchanges it for a laundry list.)

ROSINA
Grazie, grazie, grazie.

BARTOLO
Grazie, grazie, grazie un corno!
Qua quel foglio,
impertinente! A chi dico? Presto qua!

CONTE
Vuol battaglia? Attenzion...
Ih! Ah!

And friends standing here. Attention!

BARTOLO

Stop, stop...

COUNT
What is it? Ah!

BARTOLO
Let me see it.

COUNT
Yes, if it were a prescription!...
But a note...it is my duty...
If you will pardon me.

ROSINA
Thank you. Thank you.

BARTOLO
Thank you, thank you, thank you nothing!
Give me the paper,
impertinent one! Quickly, I say!

COUNT
You wish to battle? On guard...
Ih! Ah!

ROSINA

Ma quel foglio che chiedete
per azzardo m'è cascato.
È la lista del bucato.

BARTOLO

Ah, fraschetta, presto qua!
Ah, che vedo!

(Rosina gives the laundry list to Bartolo; she and the Count cross left. Berta looks through the spy hole of the street door.)

BERTA

Il barbiere...

BARTOLO

Ho preso abbaglio! È la lista!

BERTA

Quanta gente!

BARTOLO

Son di stucco!

CONTE

Bravo, bravo il mammalucco!

BARTOLO

Ah, son proprio un mammalucco,
oh, che gran bestialità!

(Basilio enters, singing from a sheet of music.)

BASILIO

Sol do re mi fa re sol mi

ROSINA

But this paper which you ask for
fell to the floor by chance.
It is only the laundry list.

BARTOLO

Oh, you flirt, come quickly here!
What do I see!

BERTA

The barber...

BARTOLO

I was mistaken! It is in the laundry list!

BERTA

So many people!

BARTOLO

I am petrified!

COUNT

Bravo, bravo, the old fool!

BARTOLO

Yes, I really am an imbecile,
oh, what a big mistake!

BASILIO

Sol do re mi fa re sol mi

la fa si sol do,
ma che imbroglio è questo qua.

ROSINA E CONTE
Bravo, bravo il mammalucco
che nel sacco entrato è già.

BERTA
Non capisco, son di stucco,
qualche imbroglio qui ci sta.

ROSINA *(alla fontana, che piange)*
Ecco qua! Sempre un'istoria,
sempre oppressa e maltrattata!
Ah, che vita disperata!
Non la so più sopportar.

BARTOLO
Ah, Rosina poverina...

CONTE

(chases Bartolo away. The others try to restrain him.)

Tu vien qua, cosa le hai fatto?

BARTOLO
Ah, fermate...niente affatto...

CONTE
Ah, canaglia, traditore...

**ROSINA, BERTA, BARTOLO E
BASILIO**
Via, fermatevi, signore.

la fa si sol do,
but what confusion this is here.

ROSINA AND COUNT
Bravo, bravo, the old fool;
in the trap at last he is caught.

BERTA
I am petrified, bewildered,
what confusion this is here.

ROSINA *(at the fountain, weeping)*
Once again! The same old story,
I am always oppressed and mistreated!
What a wretched life I live!
I can't stand it any more.

BARTOLO
Ah, poor little Rosina.

COUNT

Come here, what have you done to her?

BARTOLO
Stop...nothing at all...

COUNT
You cur, you traitor...

**ROSINA, BERTA, BARTOLO AND
BASILIO**
Hands off, away, sir.

CONTE
Io ti voglio subissar.

COUNT
I'd like to knock you down.

ROSINA E BERTA
Gente, aiuto...ma chetatevi...
Gente, aiuto...per pietà!

ROSINA AND BERTA
Good people, help...but calm yourself...
Good people, help...for mercy's sake!

BARTOLO E BASILIO
Gente, aiuto...soccorretemi...
Gente, aiuto...per pietà!

BARTOLO AND BASILIO
Good people, help...help me!
Good people, help...for mercy's sake!

CONTE
Lasciatemi, lasciatemi!

COUNT
Unhand me, unhand me!

(Figaro enters with a basin under his arm.)

FIGARO
Alto là!
Che cosa accadde, signori miei,
che chiasso è questo? Eterni dei!
Già sulla strada a questo strepito...
S'è radunata mezza città.

FIGARO
Stop!
What is happening,
what clamour is this? Great gods!
This uproar into the streets
has drawn half the city.

(softly to the Count)

Signor, giudizio, per carità.

For Heaven's sake, be careful, sir.

BARTOLO *(additando il Conte)*
Quest'è un bribante...

BARTOLO *(pointing to the Count)*
This is the rascal.

CONTE *(additando Bartolo)*
Quest'è un briccone.

COUNT *(pointing to Bartolo)*
This is the scoundrel!

BARTOLO
Ah, disgraziato!

BARTOLO
Oh, what a villain!

CONTE	**COUNT**
Ah, maledetto!	Oh, what a cursed fellow!
FIGARO	**FIGARO**
Signor soldato, porti rispetto,	Signor Soldier, have respect,
o questo fusto, corpo del diavolo,	or this basin soon shall teach you
or la creanza le insegnerà.	of your manners to beware.
(Signor, giudizio, per carità.)	(For Heaven's sake, be careful, sir.)
CONTE	**COUNT**
Brutto scimmiotto...	Ugly baboon...
BARTOLO	**BARTOLO**
Birbo malnato...	Low-born scoundrel...
ROSINA, BERTA, FIGARO E BASILIO	**ROSINA, BERTA, FIGARO AND BASILIO**
Zitto, dottore...	Be quiet, doctor...
BARTOLO	**BARTOLO**
Voglio gridare...	I'll shout it loud...
ROSINA, BERTA, FIGARO E BASILIO	**ROSINA, BERTA, FIGARO AND BASILIO**
Fermo, signore...	Hold, sir...
CONTE	**COUNT**
Voglio ammazzare...	I am going to murder...
ROSINA, BERTA, FIGARO E BASILIO	**ROSINA, BERTA, FIGARO AND BASILIO**
Fate silenzio, per carità!	Be silent, for pity's sake!
CONTE	**COUNT**
No, voglio ucciderlo,	I'm going to kill him
non v'è pietà.	without mercy.
ROSINA, BERTA, FIGARO E BASILIO	**ROSINA, BERTA, FIGARO AND BASILIO**
Fate silenzio, per carità!	Be silent, for pity's sake!

(loud knocking on the door)

ROSINA, BERTA E FIGARO
Zitti, ché bussano...

ROSINA, BERTA AND FIGARO
Silence, they are knocking.

TUTTI
Che mai sarà?

ALL
Who can it be?

BARTOLO *(guardando in strada)*
Chi è?

BARTOLO *(looking out into the street)*
Who's there?

CORO *(da fuori)*
La forza, la forza, aprite qua!

CHORUS *(from without)*
Open the door in the name of the law!

TUTTI
La forza! oh, diavolo!

ALL
The police! Oh, the devil!

FIGARO E BASILIO
L'avete fatta!

FIGARO AND BASILIO
Now you have done it!

CONTE E BARTOLO
Niente paura! Venga pur qua.

COUNT AND BARTOLO
Have no fear! Let them come in.

TUTTI
Quest'avventura, ah!
come diavolo mai finirà!

ALL
I wonder how on earth
this adventure will end!

(An officer, soldiers and townspeople burst into the courtyard.)

CORO
Fermi tutti. Nessun si mova.
Miei signori, che si fa?
Questo chiasso donde è nato?
La cagione presto qua.

CHORUS
Stay where you are. Let no one move.
Good sirs, what's going on?
What is the cause of this disturbance?
Quickly give an explanation.

BARTOLO

Questa bestia di soldato,
mio signor, m'ha maltrattato,
sì, signor, sì, signor.

FIGARO

Io qua venni, mio signore,
questo chiasso ad acquetar.
Sì, signor, sì, signor.

BASILIO E BERTA

Fa un inferno di rumore,
parla sempre d'ammazzar,
sì, signor, sì, signor.

CONTE

In alloggio quel briccone
non mi volle qui accettar.
Sì, signor, sì, signor.

ROSINA

Perdonate, poverino,
tutto effetto fu del vino.
Sì, signor, sì, signor.

UFFICIALE

Ho inteso, ho inteso.

(to the Count)

Galantuom, siete in arresto.
Fuori presto, via di qua.

CONTE

In arresto? Io? fermi, olà!

BARTOLO

This dog of a soldier,
good sir, has mistreated me,
Yes, sir, yes, sir.

FIGARO

I only came, good sir,
to calm this disturbance.
Yes, sir, yes, sir.

BASILIO AND BERTA

He is making an infernal noise,
he is threatening to kill us,
yes, sir, yes, sir.

COUNT

As a lodger, this villain
is not willing to accept me.
Yes, sir, yes, sir.

ROSINA

Pardon him, poor fellow,
he is affected by wine.
Yes, sir, yes, sir.

OFFICER

I heard you, I heard you.

My good man, you are under arrest.
Quickly come away from here.

COUNT

Arrested? I? Stop now!

(The Count presents a document to the officer who, after reading it, salutes smartly; the soldiers present arms. All remain astonished.)

<table>
<tr><td>

ROSINA

Fredda ed immobile
come una statua,
fiato non restami
da respirar.

</td><td>

ROSINA

Cold and motionless
like a statue,
I have hardly
breath to breathe!

</td></tr>
</table>

DISC NO. 2/TRACKS 4 & 5

Fredda ed immobile...Ma signor...Ma un dottore. Everything you have heard so far prepares you for one of the most exuberant and delicious events in the entire operatic literature—a bustling Rossini ensemble that brings down the first act curtain. There is a deceptively calm beginning (Track 4), in which the characters sing of how they are so stupefied by the turn of events they can barely breathe. A gravely beautiful turn of phrase in the orchestra (03:07) is dashed with a sudden realization by the characters that they must do something, anything. And they do (Track 5), madly going in all directions until the chaos is too much. To a person, they protest their confusion (00:25), which only gets worse (01:02). It grows into a whirling frenzy (01:28), receding a bit, only to start up again (02:17). The frenzy returns inevitably (03:17), sounding even crazier, as the first act careens to a madcap finish with Rosina's sparkling high notes merrily crowning the ensemble.

<table>
<tr><td>

CONTE

Freddo ed immobile
come una statua,
fiato non restagli
da respirar!

</td><td>

COUNT

Cold and motionless
like a statue,
she has hardly
breath to breathe!

</td></tr>
<tr><td>

BARTOLO

Freddo ed immobile
come una statua,
fiato non restami
da respirar!

</td><td>

BARTOLO

Cold and motionless
like a statue,
I have hardly
breath to breathe!

</td></tr>
</table>

FIGARO

Guarda Don Bartolo,
sembra una statua!
Ah, ah, dal ridere
sto per crepar!

BASILIO

Freddo ed immobile,
fiato non restami
da respirar!

BERTA

Fiato non restami
da respirar!

BARTOLO

Ma signor...ma un dottor...
ma se lei...ma vorrei...
ma se noi...ma se poi...
ma sentite, ascolate...

CORO

Zitto, tu! Oh, non più!
Non parlar, non gridar.
Zitti voi! Pensiam noi.
Zitto tu! Non parlar.
Vada ognun pei fatti suoi.
Si finisca d'altercar!

ROSINA E BASILIO

Ma se noi...ma se poi...
ma se poi...ma se noi...
Zitto su! Zitto giù!
Zitto qua! Zitto là!

FIGARO

Look at Don Bartolo,
he stands like a statue!
Oh, I am ready
to burst with laughter!

BASILIO

Cold and motionless,
I have hardly
breath to breathe!

BERTA

I have hardly
breath to breathe!

BARTOLO

But sir...for a doctor...
But if you...but I would like...
but if we...but if then...
but listen, but hear...

CHORUS

Silence all! That's enough!
Do not speak, do not shout.
Silence! We'll take care of it.
Silence you! Do not speak.
Everybody go about their business.
An end to the quarrelling!

ROSINA AND BASILIO

But if we...but if then...
but if then...but if we...
Silence here! Silence there!
Silence, silence everywhere!

BERTA, CONTE E FIGARO

Zitto su! Zitto giù!

Zitto qua! Zitto là!

TUTTI

Mi par d'esser con la testa

in un'orrida fucina,

dove cresce e mai non resta

dell'incudini sonore

l'importuno strepitar.

Alternando questo e quello,

pesantissimo martello,

fa con barbara armonia

mure e volte rimbombar.

E il cervello poverello,

già stordito, sbalordito,

non ragiona, si confonde,

si riduce ad impazzar.

BERTA, COUNT AND FIGARO

Silence here! Silence there!

Silence, silence everywhere!

ALL

My head seems to be

in a fiery smithy:

the sound of the anvils

ceaseless and growing

deafens the ear.

Up and down, high and low,

striking heavily, the hammer

makes the very walls resound

with a barbarous harmony.

Thus our poor, bewildered brain,

stunned, confounded,

in confusion, without reason,

is reduced to insanity.

Act 2

The music room in Dr Bartolo's house.

DISC NO.2/TRACK 6

Act II begins quietly, with a few notes on the harpsichord and Bartolo, alone, muttering to himself.

BARTOLO *(solo)*

Ma vedi il mio destino!
Quel soldato,
per quanto abbia cercato,
niun lo conosce
in tutto il reggimento.
Io dubito...eh, cospetto...
Che dubitar? Scommetto
che dal Conte Almaviva
è stato qui spedito quel signore
ad esplorar della Rosina il core.
(Pesta il piede furiosamente.)
Nemmeno in casa propria
sicuri si può star! Ma io...
(Si sente bussare alla porta principale.)
Chi batte? Ehi, chi è di là!
Battono, non sentite?
In casa io son,
non v'è timore, asprite.

BARTOLO *(alone)*

Look at my ill-fortune!
That soldier,
as far as I can learn,
is known by nobody
in the whole regiment.
I doubt...oh, damnation...
Did I say doubt? I would wager
that the Count Almaviva
has sent this fellow here
to sound out Rosina's heart.
(Angrily he stamps his foot.)
Not even in one's own house
can one be safe! But I...
(Knocks are heard at the main door.)
Who is knocking? Eh, who is there!
They are knocking, don't you hear?
I am home,
have no fear, open.

(The Count enters disguised as a music master.)

The Count's entrance is accompanied by a very formal, repetitive tune, appropriate for a music master and even a bit annoying. The Count enhances this illusion with a nasal, pedantic disguised voice as he repeats himself for the next few minutes, eliciting comical echoes from Bartolo.

CONTE
Pace e gioia sia con voi.

COUNT
Peace and happiness be with you.

BARTOLO
Mille grazie, non s'incomodi.

BARTOLO
A thousand thanks, come right in.

CONTE
Gioia e pace per mill'anni.

COUNT
Happiness and peace for a thousand years.

BARTOLO
Obbligato in verità.
(Questo volto non m'è ignoto.
Non ravviso, non ricordo,
ma quel volto, ma quel volto...
Non capisco, chi sarà?)

BARTOLO
In truth I am obliged to you.
(That face is not unknown to me.
I don't recall, I don't remember,
but that face, that face...
I do not know, who can it be?)

CONTE
(Ah, se un colpo è andato a vuoto
a gabbar questo balordo
un novel travestimento
più propizio a me sarà.)
Gioia e pace sia con voi.

COUNT
(Ah, if before I failed
to deceive this simpleton,
my new disguise should prove
more successful.)
Peace and happiness be with you.

BARTOLO
Ho capito! (Oh, ciel! Che noia!)

BARTOLO
I heard you! (Heavens, what a bore!)

CONTE
Gioia e pace, ben di core.

COUNT
Happiness and peace, from my heart.

BARTOLO

Basta, basta, per pietà.

BARTOLO

Enough, enough, for pity's sake.

CONTE

Gioia...

COUNT

Happiness...

BARTOLO

Gioia...

BARTOLO

Happiness...

CONTE

Pace...

COUNT

Peace...

BARTOLO

Pace...Ho capito! (Oh ciel! Che noia!)

BARTOLO

Peace...I heard you! (What a bore!)

CONTE

Ben di core, pace e gioia.

COUNT

From my heart, peace and happiness.

BARTOLO

Pace a gioia. Basta, basta, per pietà!
(Ma che perfido destino!
Ma che barbara giornata!
Tutti quanti a me davanti!
Che crudel fatalità!)

BARTOLO

Peace and happiness. Enough, for pity's sake!
(What a wretched fate is mine!
What a terrible day this is!
Everyone against me!
What a cruel destiny!)

CONTE

(Il vecchion non mi conosce,
oh, mia sorte fortunata!
Ah, mio ben! Fra pochi istanti
parlerem con libertà!

COUNT

(The old fellow knows me not.
How fortunate for me!
Ah, my love! In a few moments
we shall be able to speak freely!)

DISC NO. 2/TRACKS 8 & 9

The Count maintains his disguise (and funny voice) as he develops a counter-plot with Basilio.

BARTOLO

(hastening to prevent the Count from starting all over again)

Insomma, mio signore, chi è lei?
Si può sapere?

CONTE
Don Alonso, professore di musica
ed allievo di Don Basilio.

BARTOLO
Ebbene?

CONTE
Don Basilio sta male, il poverino,
ed in sua vece...

BARTOLO
Sta mal? Corro a vederlo.

CONTE
Piano, piano. Non è mal così grave.

BARTOLO
(Di costui non mi fido.)
Andiamo, andiamo.

CONTE
Ma signore...

BARTOLO
Cosa c'è?

CONTE
Voleva dirvi...

BARTOLO

In a word, sir, who are you?
May one know?

COUNT
Don Alonso, teacher of music
and pupil of Don Basilio.

BARTOLO
Well?

COUNT
Don Basilio, poor man, is taken ill,
and in his stead...

BARTOLO
Taken ill? I'll go and see him at once.

COUNT
Take it easy. His illness is not that serious.

BARTOLO
(I don't trust this fellow.)
Come, let us go.

COUNT
But sir...

BARTOLO
Well, what?

COUNT
I wished to say...

BARTOLO

Parlate forte.

CONTE *(sottovoce)*

Ma...

BARTOLO

Forte, vi dico.

CONTE

Ebben, come volete,

ma chi sia Don Alonso apprenderete.

(raising his voice)

Vo' dal Conte Almaviva...

BARTOLO

Piano, piano, dite, dite.

V'ascolto.

CONTE

Il Conte...

BARTOLO

Pian, per carità!

CONTE

Stamane, nella stessa locanda

era meco d'alloggio,

ed in mie mani, per caso

(dando a Bartolo una lettera di Rosina)

capitò questo biglietto

della vostra pupilla

a lui direutto.

BARTOLO

Speak up.

COUNT *(sottovoce)*

But...

BARTOLO

Speak up, I tell you.

COUNT

Well, as you wish.

Then you shall learn who Don Alonso is.

I come from Count Almaviva...

BARTOLO

Softly, softly, speak, speak.

I am listening.

COUNT

The Count...

BARTOLO

Softly, for goodness' sake!

COUNT

This morning I met him in the same inn

where I was lodging,

and into my hand, by chance,

(giving Bartolo one of Rosina's letters)

fell this note,

addressed by your ward

to him.

BARTOLO

Che vedo? È sua scrittura!

CONTE

Don Basilio nulla sa di quel foglio,
ed io, per lui venendo
a dar lezione alla ragazza,
volvea farmene un merito con voi...
perché con quel biglietto...si potrebbe...

BARTOLO

Che cosa?

CONTE

Vi dirò...s'io potessi
parlare alla ragazza, io creder...
verbigrazia...le farei
che me lo die' del Conte un'altra amante,
prova significante
che il Conte di Rosina si fa gioco,
e perciò...

BARTOLO

Piano un poco...Una calunnia!
Oh, bravo, degno e vero scolar
di Don Basilio!
Io saprò, come merita, ricompensar
sì bel suggerimento. Vo' a chiamar
la ragazza. Poiché tanto per me
v'interessate, mi raccomando a voi.

CONTE

Non dubitate.

(Bartolo goes to fetch Rosina.)

BARTOLO

What do I see! It is her writing!

COUNT

Don Basilio knows nothing of this paper,
and I, coming instead of him
to give lessons to the young lady,
wished to acquire merit in your eyes
because with this note...one could...

BARTOLO

Could what?

COUNT

I shall tell you...If I could only
speak with the girl, I could...
with your permission...make her believe
that it was given to me by a mistress
of the Count, clear proof
that the Count is playing with her affection,
and therefore...

BARTOLO

Softly...A calumny!
Oh, you are indeed a worthy pupil
of Don Basilio!
I shall know how to reward you
as you deserve for this happy suggestion.
I'll call the girl. Since you show
so much interest, I trust myself to you.

COUNT

Do not worry.

L'affare del biglietto
dalla bocca m'è uscito non volendo.
Ma come far? Senza un tal ripiego,
mi toccava andar via come un baggiano.
Il mio disegno
a lei ora paleserò;
s'ella acconsente,
io son felice appieno.
Eccola. Ah, il cor sento
balzarmi in seno!

This affair of the note
was a slip of the tongue.
But what was I to do? Without some trick,
I would have had to leave like a fool.
I must now acquaint her
with my plan;
if she consents,
I shall be a happy man.
Here she is. Oh, how my heart
is beating in my breast!

(Bartolo returns leading Rosina by the hand.)

BARTOLO
Venite, signorina.
Don Alonso, che qui vedete,
or vi darà lezione.

BARTOLO
Come, Signorina.
Don Alonso, whom you see,
will give you your lesson.

ROSINA *(vedendo il Conte)*
Ah!

ROSINA *(recognizing the Count)*
Ah!

BARTOLO
Cos'è stato?

BARTOLO
What's the matter?

ROSINA
È un granchio al piede.

ROSINA
Oh...a cramp in my foot.

CONTE *(conducendola al clavicembalo)*
Oh, nulla! Sedete a me vicin,
bella fanciulla. Se non vi spiace
un poco di lezione
di Don Basilio invece vi darò.

COUNT *(taking her to the harpsichord)*
Oh, it's nothing! Sit by my side,
fair young lady. If you don't mind,
in place of Don Basilio,
I shall give you a short lesson.

ROSINA
Oh, con mio gran piacere la prenderò.

ROSINA
Oh, with the greatest of pleasure.

CONTE	COUNT
Che volete cantar?	What would you like to sing?

ROSINA	ROSINA
Io canto, se le aggrada,	I shall sing, if you please,
il rondò dell'Inutil precauzione.	the rondo from The Futile Precaution.

BARTOLO	BARTOLO
Eh, sempre, sempre in bocca	Oh, you're always prating
L'Inutil precauzione!	about The Futile Precaution.

ROSINA	ROSINA
Io ve l'ho detto:	I told you:
è il titolo dell'opera novella.	it's the title of the new opera.

BARTOLO	BARTOLO
Orbene, intesi; andiamo.	Very well, Iunderstand; come now.

ROSINA	ROSINA
Eccolo qua.	Here it is.

CONTE	COUNT
Da brava, incominciamo.	Good, let's begin.

(He sits down at the harpsichord and accompanies Rosina.)

DISC NO. 2/TRACK 10

The "Music Lesson" scene was lost for many years, leading to the tradition of sopranos inter-polating arias and even popular songs at this point in the opera. This recording uses the newly rediscovered, shamelessly "showy" music Rossini composed for this scene.

ROSINA	ROSINA
Contro un cor che accende amore	Against a heart inflamed with love,
di verace invitto ardore,	burning with unquenchable fire,

s'arma invan poter tiranno
di rigor, di crudeltà.
D'ogni assalto vincitore,
sempre amore trionferà.

(Bartolo has gone to sleep in the armchair.)

Ah, Lindoro, mio tesoro.
Se sapessi, se vedessi,
questo cane di tutore,
ah, che rabbia che mi fa!
Caro, a te mi raccomando,
tu mi salva, per pietà!

CONTE
Non temer, ti rassicura,
sorte amica a noi sarà.

ROSINA
Dunque spero?

CONTE
A me t'affida.

ROSINA
E il mio cor?

CONTE
Giubilerà!

ROSINA
Cara immagine ridente,
dolce idea d'un lieto amor,
tu m'accendi in petto, il core.
Tu mi porti a delirar!

a ruthless tyrant, cruelly armed,
wages war, but all in vain.
From every attack a victor,
Love will always triumph.

Ah, Lindoro, my dearest treasure!
If you could know, if you could see
this dog of a guardian,
oh, I rage to think of him!
Dearest, in you I put my trust,
please, come save me, for pity's sake!

COUNT
Fear not, be reassured,
fate will be our friend.

ROSINA
Then I may hope?

COUNT
Trust in me.

ROSINA
And my heart?

COUNT
It will rejoice!

ROSINA
Dear smiling image,
sweet thought of happy love,
you burn in my breast, in my heart.
I am delirious with joy!

Caro, a te mi raccomando,	Dearest, in you I put my trust,
tu mi salva, per pietà!	please, come save me, for pity's sake!
tu mi porti a delirar!	I am delirious with joy!

DISC NO. 2/TRACKS 11-13

Bartolo shows his contempt for the "new" music (and, by implication, for Rosina's obvious desire to have a young husband) by attempting to sing an aria (track 12) in the style of the previous generation. Caffariello was a great castrato (1710 – 1783) who starred in the operas of Rossini's predecessors. Rossini thus delightfully equates conservative music critics who disliked his innovative operas with foolish old men who think they should woo young ladies. Figaro's entrance (track 13) makes fun of Bartolo, since Figaro was understood as the "new man for the new era."

CONTE

Bella voce! Bravissima!

COUNT

A beautiful voice! Bravissima!

ROSINA

Oh! Mille grazie!

ROSINA

Oh! A thousand thanks!

BARTOLO

BARTOLO

(waking up and crossing to harpsichord)

Certo, bella voce!	Truly, a beautiful voice!
Ma quest'aria, cospetto!	But this aria, damnation!
è assai noiosa.	It is rather tiresome.
La musica a' miei tempi	Music in my day
era altra cosa.	was quite another thing.
Ah! Quando, per esempio, cantava	Ah! When, for instance,
Caffariello quell'aria portentosa...	Caffariello sang that wonderful aria...
La ra la la la...sentite,	la ra la la la...Listen,
Don Alonso, eccola qua.	Don Alonso, here it is.
"Quando mi sei vicina,	"When you are near me,
amabile Rosina..."	Sweet Rosina..."

(Figaro enters and hides behind Bartolo.)

L'aria dicea "Giannina",	The aria says "Giannina,"
ma io dico "Rosina..."	but I say "Rosina..."
"Quando mi sei vicina,	"When you are near me,
amabile Rosina,	sweet Rosina,
il cor mi brilla in petto.	my heart glows in my breast,
Mi balla il minuetto..."	it dances a minuet..."

(He dances a courtly step. He notices the presence of Figaro who is imitating him behind his back.)

Bravo, signor barbiere, ma bravo!   Bravo, signor Barber, bravo!

FIGARO
Eh, niente affatto, scusi,
son debolezze...

FIGARO
Excuse me please,
it was a moment of weakness...

BARTOLO
Ebben, guidone, che vieni a fare?

BARTOLO
Well, you rascal, what are you here for?

FIGARO
Oh, bella! Vengo a farvi la barba!
Oggi vi tocca.

FIGARO
Here for! Here to shave you.
This is your day.

BARTOLO
Oggi non voglio.

BARTOLO
I don't wish it today.

FIGARO
Oggi non vuol?
Dimani non potrò io.

FIGARO
Today you don't wish it?
Tomorrow I can't come.

BARTOLO
Perché?

BARTOLO
Why not?

FIGARO *(consultando il suo diario)*

Perché ho da fare.

A tutti gli Uffiziali

del nuovo reggimento

barba e testa,

alla Marchesa Andronica

il biondo parruchin

coi maroné...

Al Contino Bombè

il ciuffo a campanile...

Purgante all'avvocato Bernardone

che ieri s'ammalò d'indigestione.

E poi...e poi...che serve?

Doman non posso.

BARTOLO

Orsù, meno parole.

Oggi non vo' far barba.

FIGARO

No? Cospetto! Guardate che avventori!

Vengo stamane, in casa v'è l'inferno...

Ritorno dopo pranzo...

Oggi non voglio.

per un qualche barbier da contadini?

Ma che? M'avete preso

Chiamate pur un altro.

(pretending to leave)

Io me ne vado.

BARTOLO

(Che serve? A modo suo.

Vedi che fantasia!)

FIGARO *(consulting his notebook)*

Because I shall be busy.

For all the officers

of the new regiment,

shave and haircut...

For the Marchioness Andronica,

her blond wig

tinted brown...

For the young Count Bombè,

forelock to curl...

A purge for the lawyer Bernardone

who yesterday fell ill with indigestion.

And then...and then...but why continue?

Tomorrow I cannot come.

BARTOLO

Come, less chatter.

Today I do not want to be shaved.

FIGARO

No? Nice kind of customers I have!

I come this morning, and I find a

madhouse...

I return after lunch...

What do you think? Do you take me

Today I don't want you!

for some country barber?

Find yourself another.

I am going.

BARTOLO

(What can one do? That's how he is.

He is really a character!)

(calling him back and holding out a bunch of keys to him)

Va in camera a pigliar la biancheria.	Go into the next room and bring the towels.
No, vado io stesso.	No, I'll go myself.

(He snatches back the bunch of keys before Figaro can take them.)

FIGARO

(Ah, se mi dava in mano
il mazzo delle chiavi
ero a cavallo.) Dite,

FIGARO

Oh, if I had those keys
in my hand
I should be riding high. Tell me,

(to Rosina)

non è fra quelle
la chiave che apre quella gelosia?

among the keys, isn't there the one
which opens the outside window?

ROSINA

Sì, certo. È la più nuova.

ROSINA

Yes, indeed. It is the newest.

(Bartolo returns.)

BARTOLO

(Ah, son pur buono
a lasciar quel diavol di barbiere!)
Animo, va tu stesso.

BARTOLO

(Oh, what a fool I was
to leave that devil of a barber here!)
Here, go yourself.

(He gives the keys to Figaro.)

Passato il corridor, sopra l'armadio
il tutto troverai.
Bada, non toccar nulla.

Go down the corridor, and on the shelf
you'll find everything.
Take care, don't touch anything.

FIGARO

Eh! Non son matto.

FIGARO

Oh! I know what I am doing.

(Allegri!) Vado e torno.
(Il colpo è fatto!)

(Brilliant!) I'll be right back.
(The trick has worked!)

(He goes out.)

BARTOLO *(prendendo da parte il Conte)*
È quel briccon che al Conte
ha portato il biglietto di Rosina...

BARTOLO *(taking the Count aside)*
That is the rascal who took
Rosina's letter to the Count...

CONTE
Mi sembra un imbroglion di prima sfera.

COUNT
He looks like an intriguer of the first order.

BARTOLO
Ehi! A me non me la ficca...

BARTOLO
He can't deceive me...

(A great noise is heard without.)

Ah, disgraziato me!

Oh, misery me!

ROSINA
Ah, che rumore!

ROSINA
What a crash!

BARTOLO
Oh, che briccon!
Me lo diceva il core!

BARTOLO
Oh, that rascal!
I felt my heart misgive me!

(Bartolo goes out.)

CONTE
Quel Figaro è un grand'uomo!

COUNT
That Figaro is a great man!

(to Rosina)

Or che siam soli, ditemi, o cara,
il vostro al mio destino

Now that we are alone, tell me dearest,
are you content to put your destiny

d'unir siete contenta?
Franchezza!

in my hands?
Be frank now!

ROSINA
Ah! mio Lindoro, altro
io non bramo...

ROSINA
Ah, Lindoro, it is
my only desire...

(Bartolo and Figaro return.)

CONTE
Ebben?

COUNT
Well?

BARTOLO
Tutto m'ha rotto, sei piatti,
otto bicchieri, una terrina.

BARTOLO
He has broken everything, six plates,
eight glasses, a tureen.

FIGARO
Vedete che gran cosa!

FIGARO
What good luck!

(Secretly he shows the Count the key of the balcony window which he has taken.)

Ad una chiave se io non m'attaccava
per fortuna, per quel maledettissimo corridor
così oscuro, spezzato mi sarei
la testa al muro. Tiene ogni stanza
al buio...e poi...

If I had not held on to a key
I would have broken my head
in that cursed corridor.
He keeps every room
so dark...and then...

BARTOLO
Oh, non più...

BARTOLO
Enough of this...

FIGARO
Dunque andiam.

FIGARO
Then let's get going.

(to the Count and Rosina)

(Giudizio.)	(Be careful.)

(Bartolo prepares to be shaved.)

BARTOLO

A noi.

BARTOLO

Now to business.

(Don Basilio enters.)

DISC NO. 2/TRACK 14

Don Basilio!...Cosa veggo. The whole ruse threatens to come crashing down with the arrival of the real Don Basilio. Rossini treats the moment as a rollicking, virtuosic ensemble set-piece; hearing it is like watching an intricate machine with hundreds of parts, all running smoothly. Listen, at any random moment, to the way the musical line captures the emotion or intention of what the character sings. The orchestral accompaniment is deft and simple, keeping the action of the characters in the forefront. Basilio finally announces his departure, and he is bid farewell by everyone (04:26) with a sunny melody that feigns good will, though he can't leave quickly enough for them. The violins play a skittish little figure (06:50) that sets up the action that follows: Figaro shaves Bartolo, while the disguised Count and Rosina (supposedly having a music lesson) plot their departure. The transparency of the music adds shivers of excitement to the sly deceptions at work here. But Bartolo overhears (08:59), and explodes in a rage. Rossini spins out another fizzy little melody that sets up the frantic coda to the whole scene (09:20).

ROSINA

(Don Basilio!)

ROSINA

Don Basilio!

ONTE

(Cosa veggo!)

COUNT

(What do I see!)

FIGARO

(Quale intoppo!)

FIGARO

(How unfortunate!)

BARTOLO

Come qua?

BARTOLO

How come you are here?

BASILIO
Servitor, di tutti quanti.

BASILIO
At your service, one and all.

BARTOLO
(Che vuol dir tal novità?)

BARTOLO
(What is this new turn of affairs?)

ROSINA
(Di noi che mai sarà?)

ROSINA
(What will happen to us?)

CONTE E FIGARO
(Qui franchezza ci vorrà.)

COUNT AND FIGARO
(We must act boldly.)

BARTOLO
Don Basilio, come state?

BARTOLO
Don Basilio, how are you feeling?

BASILIO
Come sto?...

BASILIO
How am I feeling?

FIGARO
Or che s'aspetta?
Questa barba benedetta,
la facciamo sì o no?

FIGARO
What are you waiting for?
That blessed beard of yours,
shall I shave it or not?

BARTOLO *(a Figaro)*
Ora vengo.

BARTOLO *(to Figaro)*
In a minute.

(to Basilio)

E...il curiale?

And...the notary?

BASILIO
Il curiale...

BASILIO
The notary...

CONTE
Io gli ho narrato
che già tutto è combinato.

COUNT
I have already told him
that everything is arranged.

123

(to Bartolo)

Non è ver?	Is it not true?

BARTOLO
Sì, sì, tutto io so.

BARTOLO
Yes, yes I know it all.

BASILIO
Ma, Don Bartolo, spiegatevi...

BASILIO
But, Don Bartolo, explain to me...

CONTE

COUNT

(drawing Bartolo aside to separate him from Basilio)

Ehi, dottore, una parola...	Doctor, one word...
Don Basilio, son da voi.	Don Basilio, I'll be with you.

(to Bartolo)

Ascolate un poco qua.	Listen to me for a moment.

(aside to Figaro)

Fate un po' ch'ei vada via,	Try and get rid of him,
ch'ei ci scopra ho gran timore.	or I fear he will expose us.

ROSINA
(Io mi sento il cor tremar.)

ROSINA
I feel my heart tremble.

FIGARO
(Non vi state a disperar.)

FIGARO
Don't be alarmed.

CONTE *(a Bartolo)*
Della lettera, signore,
ei l'affare ancor non sa.

COUNT *(to Bartolo)*
Of the letter, sir,
he as yet knows nothing.

BASILIO

(Ah, qui certo v'è un pasticcio,
non s'arriva a indovinar.)

CONTE

(Ch'ei ci scopra ho gran timore;
ei l'affare ancor non sa.)

BARTOLO

(Dite bene, mio signore,
or lo mando via di qua.)

CONTE

Colla febbre, Don Basilio,
chi v'insegna colla febbre a passeggiare?

BASILIO

Colla febbre?

CONTE

E che vi pare?
Siete giallo come un morto.

BASILIO

Sono giallo come un morto?

FIGARO (tastando il polso di Basilio)

Bagatella! Cospetton!
Che tremarella!
Questa è febbre scarlattina!

BASILIO

Scarlattina!

BASILIO

(There is something going on
which I certainly cannot fathom.)

COUNT

I fear he will expose us;
he as yet knows nothing.

BARTOLO

You are right, sir.
I will immediately send him away.

COUNT

With such a fever, Don Basilio,
who told you to go out?

BASILIO

What fever?

COUNT

What do you think?
You are yellow as a corpse.

BASILIO

I am yellow as a corpse?

FIGARO (feeling Basilio's pulse)

Good Heaven, my man,
you are all of a tremble!
You must have scarlet fever!

BASILIO

Scarlet fever!

CONTE

(secretly handing Basilio a purse of money)

Via, prendete medicina.
Non vi state a rovinar.

FIGARO
Presto, presto, andate a letto.

CONTE
Voi paura inver mi fate.

ROSINA
Dice bene, andate a letto...

BARTOLO, ROSINA, CONTE E FIGARO
Presto, andate a riposar.

BASILIO
(Una borsa!...andate a letto!
Ma che tutti sian d'accordo!)

BARTOLO, ROSINA, CONTE E FIGARO
Presto a letto, presto a letto...

BASILIO
Eh, non son sordo,
non mi faccio più pregar.

FIGARO
Che color!...

COUNT

Go take some medicine.
Don't stay here and kill yourself.

FIGARO
Quickly, quickly, go to bed.

COUNT
I am really afraid for you.

ROSINA
He is right, go home to bed...

BARTOLO, ROSINA, COUNT AND FIGARO
Quickly, go and have some rest.

BASILIO
(A purse!...Go to bed!
As long as they are all of one mind!)

BARTOLO, ROSINA, COUNT AND FIGARO
Quickly to bed, quickly to bed...

BASILIO
I am not deaf,
you don't have to beg me.

FIGARO
What a colour!

CONTE
Che brutta cera!...

COUNT
You look terrible!

BASILIO
Brutta cera?

BASILIO
Terrible?

CONTE, FIGARO, E BARTOLO
Oh, brutta assai!...

COUNT, FIGARO AND BARTOLO
Oh, really terrible!

BASILIO
Dunque vado!...

BASILIO
Well, I'll go!

ROSINA, CONTE, FIGARO E BARTOLO
Vada. Vada.

ROSINA, COUNT, FIGARO AND BARTLO
Go, go.

CONTE, ROSINA E FIGARO
Buona sera, mio signore,
presto andate via di qua.

COUNT, ROSINA AND FIGARO
Well, good-night to you, dear sir,
quickly go away from here.

BASILIO
Buona sera, ben di core...
Poi diman si parlerà.

BASILIO
Well, good-night, with all my heart,
then tomorrow we shall talk.

ROSINA E FIGARO
Maledetto seccatore,
buona sera, mio signore,
pace, sonno e sanità,
buona sera, via di qua,
presto, andate via di qua.

ROSINA AND FIGARO
Cursed man, you are a nuisance!
Well, good-night to you, dear sir,
peace and slumber and good health.
Well, good-night, get out of here,
quickly go away from here.

CONTE
Buona sera, via di qua,
buona sera, mio signore,
pace, sonno e sanità,
presto andate via di qua.

COUNT
Well, good-night, away from here.
Well, good-night to you, dear sir,
peace and slumber and good health.
Quickly go away from here.

BARTOLO

Buona sera, mio signore,
pace, sonno e sanità,
presto, andate via di qua.

BASILIO

Buona sera, ben di core,
poi diman si parlerà.
Non gridate, per pietà.

(Basilio goes out.)

FIGARO

Orsù, Signor Don Bartolo.

BARTOLO

Son qua. Son qua.

(Figaro starts to shave Don Bartolo and at the same time tries to conceal the two lovers.)

Stringi. Bravissimo.

CONTE

Rosina, deh, ascoltatemi.

ROSINA

V'ascolto. Eccomi qua.

(The Count and Rosina sit on the harpsichord stool pretending to study.)

CONTE

A mezzanotte in punto
a prendervi qui siamo.
Or che la chiave abbiamo
non v'è da dubitar.

BARTOLO

Well, good-night to you, dear sir,
peace and slumber and good health.
Quickly go away from here.

BASILIO

Well, good-night, with all my heart,
then tomorrow we shall talk.
Do not shout, for pity's sake!

FIGARO

Well, signor Don Bartolo.

BARTOLO

I am here. I am here.

Pull it tight. Bravissimo.

COUNT

Rosina, listen to me.

ROSINA

I am listening. I am here.

COUNT

At midnight precisely
we'll come for you here.
And since we have the keys
there is nothing to fear.

FIGARO

Ahi! Ahi!

FIGARO

Ah! Ah!

BARTOLO

Che cosa è stato?

BARTOLO

What's the matter?

FIGARO

Un non so che nell'occhio!...
Guardate!...Non toccate...
Soffiate, per pietà!

FIGARO

Something, I don't know what,
is in my eye!...Look...Don't touch it...
Blow into it, for pity's sake!

ROSINA

A mezzanotte in punto,
anima mia, t'aspetto.
Io già l'istante affretto
che a te mi stringerà.

ROSINA

At midnight precisely,
my love, I shall await you.
May the moments hasten
which draw you to me.

(Bartolo has become suspicious of the music lesson; he creeps over to the harpsichord while the Count is singing.)

CONTE

Ora avvertir vi voglio,
cara, che il vostro foglio,
perché non fosse inutile
il mio travestimento...

COUNT

But now I must tell you,
dearest, that your letter,
in order that I might succeed
in my disguise...

BARTOLO

Il suo travestimento?

BARTOLO

In his disguise?

(The Count and Rosina jump up and retreat around the harpsichord.)

Ah! Bravi, bravissimo!
Signor Alonso, bravo! bravi!
Bricconi! Birbanti!
Ah! voi tutti quanti
avete giurato di farmi crepar.

Ah! Bravi, bravissimi!
Signor Alonso, bravo! Bravi!
Rascals! Scoundrels!
Ah! I can see you have all sworn
to hasten my end.

(He chases all three around the room.)

Su, fuori, furfanti,	Out, you villains,
vi voglio accoppar!	or I shall kill you!

ROSINA, CONTE E FIGARO	**ROSINA, COUNT AND FIGARO**
La testa vi gira,	Your head is spinning,
ma zitto, dottore,	hush, good doctor,
vi fate burlar.	you are making a fool of yourself.
Tacete, tacete,	Be quiet, be quiet,
non serve gridare.	it's senseless to shout.
L'amico delira.	This man is delirious.
(Intesi già siamo,	(Now that it's settled
non vo' replicar.)	I don't have to repeat.)
Non serve gridar.	It is senseless to shout.

BARTOLO	**BARTOLO**
Bricconi! birbanti!	Rascals, scoundrels!
Su, fuori, furfanti,	Out, you villains,
vi voglio accoppare.	or I shall kill you!
Avete giurato di farmi crepare.	You have all sworn to hasten my end.
Di rabbia, di sdegno,	I'm fairly bursting
mi sento crepare,	with anger and disdain.
vi voglio accoppar.	I shall kill you!

(Bartolo has won the battle. The Count and Figaro run out of the house, Bartolo follows them, and Rosina escapes to her room. Berta enters.)

DISC NO. 2/TRACKS 15 & 16

Il vecchiotto cerca moglie. Berta comments on the goings-on in the "crazy house" in this scene that is often cut in performance. It is an excellent vehicle for a mezzo-soprano with comedic talents to portray the old maid who imparts a little wisdom, complains, and who wouldn't mind a little of the excitement for herself.

BERTA

Che vecchio sospettoso!

Vada pure e ci stia finché crepa!

Sempre gridi e tumulti in questa casa...

Si litiga...si piange...si minaccia...

Sì, non v'è un'ora di pace

con questo vecchio avaro e brontolone.

Oh che casa in confusione!

(She begins to tidy the room.)

Il vecchiotto cerca moglie,

vuol marito la ragazza,

quello freme, questa è pazza,

tutti e due son da legar.

Ma che cosa è quest'amore

che fa tutti delirar?

Egli è un male universale,

una smania, un pizzicore,

un solletico, un tormento,

poverina, anch'io lo sento

né so come finirà.

Oh, vecchietta maledetta!

Son da tutti disprezzata,

e vecchietta disperata

mi convien così crepar.

(Berta goes out. Bartolo enters with Basilio.)

BERTA

What a suspicious old man!

Be gone and don't come back alive!

Always shouting and clamour in this house...

Arguing...weeping...threatening...

There is not an hour's peace

with this stingy, grumbling old man.

Oh, what a house of confusion!

The old man seeks a wife,

and the maiden wants a husband,

the one is frenzied, the other crazy,

both of them need restraining.

What on earth is all this love

which makes everyone go mad?

It is a universal evil,

it is a mania and an itch,

a thing which tickles and torments you.

Unhappy me, I also feel it

and do not know how to escape.

Oh, accursed old maid!

By all I am despised,

an old maid without a hope,

I shall die in desperation.

DISC NO. 2/TRACK 17

The two old men plot in breathy recitative and convince the crestfallen Rosina of her lover's unfaithfulness.

BARTOLO

Dunque voi don Alonso

non conoscete affatto?

BASILIO

Affatto.

BARTOLO

Ah, certo. Il Conte lo mandò.

Qualche gran tradimento si prepara.

BASILIO

Io poi dico che quell'amico

era il Conte in persona.

BARTOLO

Il Conte?

BASILIO

Il Conte.

(La borsa parla chiaro.)

BARTOLO

Sia chi si vuole...

Amico, dal notaro

vo' in questo punto andare;

in questa sera stipular

di mie nozze io vo' il contratto.

BASILIO

Il notar? Siete matto?

Piove a torrenti, e poi

questa sera il notaro

è impegnato con Figaro;

il barbiere marita sua nipote.

BARTOLO

So you don't know

a Don Alonso?

BASILIO

Certainly not.

BARTOLO

Ah, of course, the Count must have sent

him. They're hatching some monstrous

plot.

BASILIO

I say that our friend

was the Count in person.

BARTOLO

The Count?

BASILIO

The Count.

(The purse he gave me speaks for itself.)

BARTOLO

I don't care who it was...

My friend, I'm off

to see the notary at once;

I'll have the marriage contract

drawn up tonight.

BASILIO

The notary! Are you mad?

It's pouring with rain. Besides,

tonight the notary

is seeing Figaro;

the barber is fixing up his niece's marriage.

BARTOLO

Una nipote? Che nipote?

Il barbiere non ha nipoti...

Ah, qui v'è qualche imbroglio.

Questa notte i bricconi

me la vogliono far;

presto, il notaro qua venga

sull'istante...

Ecco la chiave del portone:

(Bartolo gives Basilio the front door key and pushes him out.)

Andate, presto, per carità.

BASILIO

Non temete: in due salti io torno qua.

(He leaves.)

BARTOLO

Per forza o per amore Rosina

avrà da cedere.

Cospetto! Mi vien un'altra idea.

Questo biglietto che scrisse

la ragazza ad Almaviva potria servir...

Che colpo da maestro!

Don Alonso, il briccone, senza volerlo mi

diè l'armi in

mano.

Ehi! Rosina, Rosina.

(Rosina enters from her room.)

Avanti, avanti,

del vostro amante io vi vo' dar novella.

BARTOLO

His niece? What niece?

The barber has no nieces...

Aha, there's dirty work afoot.

Tonight the rogues

mean to trick me;

quick, bring the notary here

immediately...

Here's the front door key.

Hurry, hurry, for Heaven's sake.

BASILIO

Never fear: I'll be back in two shakes.

BARTOLO

Whether she likes it or not

Rosina will have to yield.

By Jove! I've another idea.

This letter the minx wrote

to Almaviva might serve...

what a masterstroke!

That rascal Don Alonso has given me the

weapon I need willy-

nilly.

Hey! Rosina, Rosina.

Come here,

I've some news of your lover for you.

Povera sciagurata!
In verità collocaste assai bene il vostro
affetto!
Del vostro amor sappiate ch'ei si fa gioco
in sen d'un'altra amante, ecco la prova.

Poor, unhappy girl!
You've certainly bestowed your affections
on a fine rascal!
You should know that he's laughing
at your love in the arms of another woman,
here's the proof.

(He shows Rosina her letter, but hangs on to it.)

ROSINA
Oh, cielo, il mio biglietto!

ROSINA
Oh, heavens, my letter!

BARTOLO
Don Alonso e il barbiere
congiuran contro voi,
non vi fidate.
Nelle braccia del Conte Almaviva
vi vogliono condurre.

BARTOLO
Don Alonso and the barber
are plotting against you,
don't trust them.
They intend to deliver
you into the arms of Count Almaviva.

ROSINA
In braccio a un altro!
Che mai sento!
Ah, Lindoro! ah, traditore!
Ah, sì!...vendetta!
E vegga quell'empio chi è Rosina.
Dite, signore, di sposarmi voi bramavate...

ROSINA
Into another's arms!
What's that you say?
Ah, Lindoro! You traitor!
Ah, so!...revenge!
This wicked one shall see who Rosina is.
Sir, you always wanted to marry me...

BARTOLO
E il voglio.

BARTOLO
And I still do.

ROSINA
Ebben, si faccia! Io son contenta!
Ma all'istante.
Udite: a mezzanotte
qui sarà l'indegno con Figaro il barbier;
con lui fuggire per sposarlo io voleva...

ROSINA
Well then, you shall! I'm...happy to.
But we must wed at once.
Listen: at midnight
the wretch will be here with Figaro, the
barber. I was going to elope with him...

BARTOLO	BARTOLO
Ah! scellerati! Corro a sbarrar la porta...	The scoundrels! I'll run and bar the door...

ROSINA	ROSINA
Ah! mio signore! Entran per la finestra.	Oh, Sir! They're going to come in through
Hanno la chiave.	the window. They've got the key.

BARTOLO	BARTOLO
Non mi muovo di qui!	I'll not budge from here!
Ma...e se fossero armati?	But...suppose they're armed.
Figlia mia, poiché ti sei	My child, as you are now
sì bene illuminata, facciam così.	so well informed, let us do this.
Chiuditi a chiave in camera,	Lock yourself in your room,
io vo' a chiamar la forza;	I'm going to call the law;
dirò che son due ladri, e come tali,	I shall say that they are two robbers and so,
corpo di Bacco! L'avremo da vedere!	the deuce! We'll see about that!
Figlia, chiuditi presto:	My child, lock yourself in:
io vado via.	I'm off.

(Bartolo runs out of the house.)

ROSINA	ROSINA
Quanto, quanto è crudel la sorte mia!	What a bitterly cruel fate is mine!

(Rosina goes to her room.)

(Storm—It is night. The balcony window is opened. Figaro and the Count wrapped in mantles enter. Figaro carries a lantern.)

DISC NO. 2/TRACK 18

The storm, depicted in the orchestra, was a commonplace of Italian opera in Rossini's time and for a long time after, used as a metaphor for human emotions of love and jealousy. There are deft reminiscences of themes from the overture (00:47) where the "tempest" erupts.

Figaro and the Count return quietly, only to find Rosina angry about her supposed deception.

FIGARO	**FIGARO**
Alfine eccoci qua.	At last we are here.
CONTE	**COUNT**
Figaro, dammi man.	Figaro, give me your hand.
Poter del mondo!	Thunder and lightning!
Che tempo indiavolato!	What wicked weather!
FIGARO	**FIGARO**
Tempo da innamorati!	What a night for lovers!

(The Count stumbles over the harpsichord stool.)

CONTE	**COUNT**
Ehi...fammi lume.	Hey...Give me some light.
Dove sarà Rosina?	Where can Rosina be?

(Rosina enters from her room. Figaro holds up his lantern.)

FIGARO	**FIGARO**
Ora vedremo...	We shall see...

(They see Rosina.)

Eccola appunto!	There she is!
CONTE	**COUNT**
Ah, mio tesoro!	Oh, my treasure!
ROSINA *(respingendolo)*	**ROSINA** *(repulsing him)*
Indietro, anima scellerata!	Stand off, wretch that you are!
Io qui di mia stolta credulità	I have come here to wipe out

venni soltanto a riparar lo scorno,
a dimostrarti qual sono
e quale amante perdesti,
anima indegna e sconoscente!

CONTE
Io son di sasso!

FIGARO
Io non capisco niente.

CONTE
Ma per pietà...

ROSINA
Taci. Fingesti amore
per vendermi alle voglie
di quel tuo vil Conte Almaviva...

CONTE
Al Conte! Ah, sei delusa!
Oh, me felice!
Adunque tu di verace amore
ami Lindor...rispondi...

ROSINA
Ah, sì!...t'amai pur troppo!

CONTE
Ah! non è tempo di più celarsi, anima mia;
ravvisa colui che sì gran tempo seguì tue
tracce, che per
te sospira, che sua ti vuole.
Mirami, o mio tesoro,
Almaviva son io, non son Lindoro.

COUNT
I am petrified!

FIGARO
I don't know what she is talking about.

COUNT
But have pity...

ROSINA
Be still. You pretended to love me
in order to sacrifice me to the lust
of the wicked Count Almaviva...

COUNT
Of the Count? Ah, you are deceived!
Oh, what happiness!
So you love Lindoro
truly...answer me...

ROSINA
Oh, yes!...I loved you too much!

COUNT
Oh, I shall keep it secret no longer, my
love; you see in me
the one who followed you for so long, who
yearns for you, who wants you to be his.
Look at me, my love,
I am Almaviva, I am not Lindoro.

Ah qual colpo inaspettato! At last, the elopement. As the briskly pulsing music suggests, the Count and Rosina could not be happier. Figaro echoes the same joyous melody, patting himself on the back for the good deeds he has done. Rosina sings an ardent new melody (02:57), which the Count takes up, while Figaro, all but rolling his eyes impatiently, argues for haste in getting away. Figaro sees someone, and he finally convinces the smitten lovers to get on— quietly, very quietly—with the business of making a getaway (04:52).

ROSINA

(Ah, qual colpo inaspettato!
Egli stesso? Oh Ciel! Che sento!
Di sorpresa e di contento
son vicina a delirar!)

FIGARO

(Son rimasti senza fiato,
ora muoion di contento,
guarda, guarda il mio talento,
che bel colpo seppe far!)

CONTE

(Qual trionfo inaspettato!
Me felice! Oh, bel momento!
Ah, d'amore e di contento
son vicino a delirar!)

FIGARO

(Son rimasti senza fiato:
ora muoion dal contento.
Guarda, guarda, guarda,
guarda il mio talento,
che bel colpo seppe far!)

ROSINA

Mio Signor!...Ma...voi...ma...io...

ROSINA

(Oh, what a shock!
It is he himself! Heavens, what do I hear?
With surprise and with joy
I am almost delirious!)

FIGARO

(They are breathless with delight,
they are dying of content,
oh, how talented I am,
what a coup I brought about!)

COUNT

(What triumph unexpected!
What a happy, wonderful moment!
With love and contentment
I am almost delirious!)

FIGARO

(They are breathless with delight,
they are dying of content.
Watch out, watch out, watch out,
how talented I am,
what a coup I brought about!)

ROSINA

My Lord!...But...you...but I...

CONTE

Ah, non più, ben mio,

il bel nome di mia sposa,

idol mio, t'attende già, sì.

ROSINA

Il bel nome di tua sposa!

Oh, qual gioia al cor mi dà!

CONTE

Sei contenta?

ROSINA

Ah! mio signore!

ROSINA E CONTE

Dolce nodo avventurato

che fai paghi i miei desiri!

Alla fin de' miei martiri

tu sentisti, amor, pietà.

FIGARO

(Nodo!) Andiamo. (Nodo!)

Presto, andiamo. (Paghi!)

Vi sbrigate.

Lasciate quei sospir.

Presto, andiam per carità.

Ah, se si tarda, i miei raggiri

fanno fiasco in verità.

Ah! Cospetto! Che ho veduto!

Alla porta una lanterna, due persone!

Che si fa?

CONTE

Hai veduto...

COUNT

You are no longer just my love,

the blessed name of wife,

adored one, awaits you.

ROSINA

The blessed name of wife!

Oh, what joy that gives my heart!

COUNT

Are you happy?

ROSINA

Oh! Good sir!

ROSINA AND COUNT

Sweet, fortunate knot,

the end of all desire!

On our sufferings,

love, you took pity.

FIGARO

(Knot!) Let's get going. (Knot!)

Quickly, Let's go. (All desire!)

Hurry up.

This is no time for sentiment.

Let's go quickly, for pity's sake.

Oh, if we delay my plans

will really come a cropper.

Oh, damnation! What do I see!

At the door a lantern, two persons!

What's to be done?

COUNT

You have seen...

FIGARO	FIGARO
Sì signor...	Yes, sir...

CONTE	COUNT
Due persone?	Two people?

(They run about in confusion.)

FIGARO	FIGARO
Sì signor...	Yes, sir...

CONTE	COUNT
Una lanterna?	A lantern?

FIGARO	FIGARO
Alla porta, sì, signor.	At the door, yes, sir.

ASSIEME	TOGETHER
Che si fa? Che si fa?	What's to be done?
Zitti, zitti, piano, piano,	Softly, softly, piano, piano,
non facciamo confusione,	no confusion, no delay,
per la scala del balcone,	by the ladder of the balcony,
presto andiamo via di qua.	quickly, let us go away.
Zitti, zitti, ecc.	Softly, softly, etc.

(Figaro leads them on to the balcony.)

DISC NO. 2/TRACK 21 & 22

The plot comes to a head—perhaps Rosina and Almaviva spent too much time "making pretty music" on track 20?

FIGARO	FIGARO
Ah, disgraziati noi! Come si fa?	Oh, how unfortunate! What's to be done?

CONTE	**COUNT**
Che avvenne mai?	What happened?
FIGARO	**FIGARO**
La scala...	The ladder...
CONTE	**COUNT**
Ebben?	Well?
FIGARO	**FIGARO**
La scala non v'è più...	The ladder is gone...
CONTE	**COUNT**
Che dici?	What do you say?
FIGARO	**FIGARO**
Chi mai l'avrà levata?	Who could have taken it away?
CONTE	**COUNT**
Qual inciampo crudel!	What a cruel blow!
ROSINA	**ROSINA**
Me sventurata!	Oh, I am so miserable!

(They run into the corner; Figaro hides the lantern under his cloak.)

FIGARO	**FIGARO**
Zi...zitti! Sento gente...	Qu...quiet, I hear people...
ora ci siamo, signor mio.	And here we are, my master.
Che si fa?	What's to be done?
CONTE	**COUNT**
Mia Rosina, coraggio!	Courage, Rosina mine!
FIGARO	**FIGARO**
Eccoli qua.	Here they are.

(Basilio enters, followed by the notary.)

BASILIO
Don Bartolo...

FIGARO
Don Basilio...

CONTE
E quell'altro?

FIGARO
Ve' ve', il nostro Notaro.
Allegramente! Lasciate fare a me...

(He comes out of hiding and lifts the lantern high.)

Signor Notaro, dovevate in mia casa
stipular questa sera il contratto
di nozze fra il Conte d'Almaviva
e mia nipote. Gli sposi eccoli qua.
Avete indosso la scrittura? Benissimo.

BASILIO
Ma piano...Don Bartolo dov'è?

CONTE
Ehi! Don Basilio,

(Calling Don Basilio aside, he takes a ring from his finger and motions to him to be silent.)

quest'anello è per voi.

BASILIO
Ma io...

BASILIO
Don Bartolo...

FIGARO
Don Basilio...

COUNT
And who is the other?

FIGARO
Oh, oh, it's our notary.
How jolly! Leave it all to me...

Signor Notary, this evening in my house
you are to settle the contract
of marriage between the Count Almaviva
and my niece. Here is the couple.
Are the papers prepared? Very good.

BASILIO
But wait...where is Don Bartolo?

COUNT
Here, Don Basilio!

This ring is for you.

BASILIO
But I...

CONTE	COUNT
Per voi vi sono ancor	For you two bullets in the head

(He plays with a loaded pistol under Basilio's nose.)

due palle nel cervello	are also waiting
se v'opponete...	if you offer any opposition...

BASILIO

Oibò! Prendo l'anello. Chi firma?

BASILIO

Dear me! I'll take the ring. Who signs?

CONTE

Eccoci qua. Son testimoni
Figaro e Don Basilio.
Essa è mia sposa.

COUNT

Here we are. Figaro and
Don Basilio are witnesses.
This is my bride.

FIGARO

Evviva!

FIGARO

Evviva!

CONTE

Oh, mio contento!

COUNT

Oh, how happy I am!

ROSINA

Oh, sospirata mia felicità!

ROSINA

Oh, this is the joy I have longed for!

FIGARO

Evviva!

FIGARO

Evviva!

(Don Bartolo enters followed by an officer and soldiers. The townspeople press into the room after him.)

BARTOLO

Fermi tutti! Eccoli qua!

BARTOLO

Halt, everyone! Here they are!

FIGARO

Colle buone, signor.

FIGARO

Gently, sir.

BARTOLO

Signor, son ladri,

arrestate, arrestate.

UFFICIALE

Mio signore, il suo nome?

CONTE

Il mio nome è quel d'un uomo d'onore.

Lo sposo io son di questa...

BARTOLO

Eh, andate al diavolo!

Rosina esser deve mia sposa: non è vero?

ROSINA

Io sua sposa?

Oh, nemmeno per pensiero.

BARTOLO

Come? Come, fraschetta?

Arrestate, vi dico,

(pointing to the Count)

è un ladro.

FIGARO

Or or l'accoppo.

BARTOLO

È un furfante, è un briccon.

UFFICIALE *(al Conte)*

Signore...

BARTOLO

Sir, they are thieves,

arrest them, arrest them.

OFFICER

Your name, sir?

COUNT

My name is that of a man of honour.

I am betrothed to this...

BARTOLO

Oh, go to the devil!

Rosina must be my bride: isn't that so?

ROSINA

I his bride?

Oh, I shouldn't dream of it.

BARTOLO

What? What's that, you hussy?

Arrest him, I tell you,

he's a thief.

FIGARO

I'll kill him on the spot.

BARTOLO

He's a knave, a rascal.

OFFICER *(to the Count)*

Sir...

CONTE	**COUNT**
Indietro!	Stand back!
UFFICIALE	**OFFICER**
Il nome?	Your name?
CONTE	**COUNT**
Indietro, dico, indietro...	Back, I say, back!...
UFFICIALE	**OFFICER**
Ehi, mio signor! Basso quel tono.	Now then, my dear Sir! Lower your voice.
Chi è lei?	Who are you?
CONTE	**COUNT**
Il Conte d'Almaviva io sono...	I am the Count Almaviva...
BARTOLO *(rassegnato)*	**BARTOLO** *(resigned)*
Insomma io ho tutti i torti...	And I'm the one who's always wrong...
FIGARO	**FIGARO**
Eh, purtroppo è così...	That's the way of things...
BARTOLO *(a Basilio)*	**BARTOLO** *(to Basilio)*
Ma tu, briccone, tu pur tradirmi	But you, you rascal, you too betrayed me
e far da testimonio!	and acted as witness!
BASILIO	**BASILIO**
Ah! Don Bartolo mio, quel signor Conte	Ah! My good Doctor Bartolo, the Count
certe ragioni ha in tasca,	has certain reasons in his pocket,
certi argomenti a cui non si risponde.	and arguments to which there is no answer.
BARTOLO *(dichiarandosi vinto)*	**BARTOLO** *(accepting defeat)*
Ed io, bestia solenne,	And I, stupid fool that I am,
per meglio assicurare il matrimonio,	the better to assure the marriage,
portai via la scala dal balcone!	took away the ladder from the balcony!

145

FIGARO

Ecco che fa un' "Inutil precauzione"!

BARTOLO

Ma...e la dote?

Io non posso...

CONTE

Eh, via, di dote io bisogno non ho:

va - te la dono.

FIGARO

Ah! Ah! ridete adesso?

Bravissimo, Don Bartolo,

ho veduto alla fin rasserenarsi

quel vostro ceffo amaro e furibondo.

Eh! i briccioni han fortuna in questo mondo.

ROSINA

Dunque, signor Don Bartolo?

BARTOLO

Sì...sì...ho capito tutto.

CONTE

Ebben, dottore?

BARTOLO

Sì...sì...che serve?

Quel ch'è fatto è fatto.

Andate pur, che il ciel vi benedica.

FIGARO

Bravo, bravo, un abbraccio,

venite qua, dottore.

FIGARO

Here is really the "Futile Precaution"!

BARTOLO

But...what about the dowry?

I cannot...

COUNT

Oh, come now, I do not need a dowry:

there...I present it to you.

FIGARO

Ha! Ha! You're laughing now?

Capital, Don Bartolo,

at last I've seen that bitter,

angry mug of yours brighten up.

Aha! Rogues are lucky in this world.

ROSINA

Well, Don Bartolo?

BARTOLO

Yes...yes...I understand perfectly.

COUNT

So...doctor?

BARTOLO

Yes...yes...what's the use?

What is done is done.

Go along with you, and may Heaven bless
you.

FIGARO

Bravo, bravo, you deserve a hug,

come here, doctor.

ROSINA	**ROSINA**
Ah, noi felici!	Oh, happy us!

CONTE	**COUNT**
Oh, fortunato amore!	Oh, fortunate love!

DISC NO. 2/TRACK 23

Di sì felice innesto Figaro. The Count and Rosina each cheer the happy turn of events, with the joyous encouragement of the chorus—another delightful Rossini finale, with Rosina again piping her delight (01:52) over the ensemble.

FIGARO	**FIGARO**
Di sì felice innesto	So happy a reunion
serbiam memoria eterna.	let us remember for ever.
Io smorzo la lanterna,	I put out my lantern,
qui più non ho che far.	I am no longer needed.

(He blows out his lamp.)

FIGARO, BARTOLO, BASILIO,	**FIGARO, BARTOLO, BASILIO, CHORUS**
CORO E BERTA *(che è entrata nel frattempo)*	**AND BERTA** *(who has entered in the meantime)*
Amor e fede eterna	May love and faith eternal
si vegga in voi regnar.	reign in both your hearts.

ROSINA E CONTE	**ROSINA AND COUNT**
Amor e fede eterna	May love and faith eternal
si vegga in noi regnar.	reign in both our hearts.

ROSINA	**ROSINA**
Costò sospiri e pene	We have hoped and sighed for
un sì felice istante:	such a happy moment.
alfin quest'alma amante	Finally this lover's soul
comincia a respirar.	begins to breathe again.

TUTTI

Amore e fede eterna
si vegga in voi regnar.

CONTE

Dell'umile Lindoro
la fiamma a te fu accetta;
più bel destin t'aspetta;
su, vieni a giubilar.

TUTTI

Amore e fede eterna
si vegga in voi regnar.

FINE

ALL

May love and faith eternal
reign in both your hearts.

COUNT

You accepted humble
Lindoro's passion.
A brighter fate awaits you,
come then and rejoice.

ALL

May love and faith eternal
reign in both your hearts.

END

All photographs are copyrighted by the photographers and in some instances by the lending institutions.

THE BARBER OF SEVILLE

Gioacchino Rossini

COMPACT DISC ONE   76:56:00

1   Overture 7:26

ATTO PRIMO/ACT ONE

2	Piano, pianissimo, senza parlar	2:57
	Fiorello/Coro/Conte	
3	Ecco ridente in cielo	4:55
	Conte	
4	Ehi? Fiorello?	1:06
	Conte/Fiorello/Coro	
5	Mille grazie, mio signore	1:48
	Coro/Conte/Fiorello	
6	Gente indescreta!	1:13
	Conte/Fiorello/Figaro	
7	La ran le ra la ran la la...Largo al factotum	4:33
	Figaro	
8	Ah, che bella vita	2:17
	Figaro/Conte	
9	Non è venuto ancora	1:54
	Rosina/Conte/Bartolo/Figaro	
10	Le vostre assidue premure...	2:34
	Figaro/Conte/Bartolo	

11	Se il mio nome saper voi bramate	2:22
	Conte/Rosina/Figaro	
12	Oh cielo!	1:02
	Conte/Figaro	
13	All'idea di quel metallo	9:07
	Figaro/Conte	
14	Una voce poco fa	5:44
	Rosina	
15	Si, si la vincerò	1:20
	Rosina/Figaro	
16	Ah, disgraziato Figaro!	1:49
	Bartolo/Rosina/Berta/Ambroglio	
17	Ah! Barbiere d'inferno	1:50
	Bartolo/Basilio	
18	La calunnia è un venticello	4:54
	Basilio	
19	Ah! Che ne dite?	0:36
	Bartolo/Basilio	
20	Ma bravi! Ma benone!	2:25
	Figaro/Rosina	
21	Dunques io son...	4:57
	Rosina/Figaro	
22	Ora me sento meglio	1:54
	Rosina/Bartolo	
23	A un dottor della mia sorte	6:06
	Bartolo	

COMPACT DISC TWO 78:14:00

1	Finora in questa camera	0:40
	Berta/Conte	
2	Ehi, di casa, buona gente...	8:22
	Conte/Bartolo/Rosina/Berta/Basilio	
3	Che cosa accadde, signori miei	3:44
	Conte/Bartolo/Rosina/Berta/Basilio/Figaro/Coro/Ufficiale	
4	Fredda ed immobile	3:20
	Rosina/Conte/Bartolo/Figaro/Basilio/Berta	
5	Ma signor...ma un dottor	4:38
	Bartolo/Coro/Rosina/Basilio/Berta/Conte/Figaro	

ATTO SECONDO/ACT TWO

6	Ma vedi il mio destino!	0:52
	Bartolo	
7	Pace e gioia sia con voi	2:50
	Conte/Bartolo	
8	Insomma, mio signore, chi è lei?	2:22
	Bartolo/Conte	
9	Venite, signorine	1:04
	Rosina/Conte/Bartolo	
10	Contro un cor che accende amore	7:32
	Rosina/Conte	
11	Bella voce! Bravissima!	0:37
	Conte/Rosina/Bartolo	
12	Quando mi sei vicina	1:02
	Bartolo	
13	Bravo, signor barbiere, ma bravo!	2:52
	Bartolo/Rosina/Figaro/Conte	
14	Don Basilio!...Cosa veggio!	11:06
	Rosina/Conte/Figaro/Bartolo/Basilio	
15	Che vecchio sospettoso!	0:30
	Berta	
16	Il vecchiotto cerca moglie	3:27
	Berta	
17	Dunque voi Don Alonso	3:45
	Bartolo/Basilio/Rosina	
18	Storm	2:58
	Orchestra	
19	Alfine eccoco qua	1:36
	Figaro/Conte/Rosina	
20	Ah, qual cual colpo inaspettato!	6:18
	Figaro/Rosina/Conte	
21	Ah, disgraziati noi!	2:23
	Figaro/Conte/Rosina/Basilio/Bartolo/Uficiale	
22	Insomma io ho tutti i torti...	1:46
	Bartolo/Figaro/Conte/Rosina	
23	Di si felice innesto	2:16
	Figaro/Bartolo/Basilio/Berta/Coro/Rosina/Conte	

THE BARBER OF SEVILLE

Gioacchino Rossini

1792 - 1868

Rosina	Beverly Sills
Il Conte d'Almaviva	Nicolai Gedda
Figaro	Sherrill Milnes
Bartolo	Renato Capecchi
Basilio	Ruggero Raimondi
Berta	Fedora Barbieri
Fiorello	Joseph Galiano
Ambrogio/Uffizialer	Michael Rippon

Conducted by James Levine
London Symphony Orchestra
John Alldis Choir
Chorus Master: John Alldis